WOMEN, BUSINESS AND THE LAW 2023

WORLD BANK GROUP

CONTENTS

Women, Business and the Law 2023 is the ninth in a series of annual studies measuring the laws that affect women's economic opportunity in 190 economies. The project presents eight indicators structured around women's interactions with the law as they progress through their lives and careers: Mobility, Workplace, Pay, Marriage, Parenthood, Entrepreneurship, Assets, and Pension.

Women, Business and the Law 2023 identifies barriers to women's economic participation and encourages the reform of discriminatory laws. This year, the study also includes new research, a literature review, and analysis of 53 years of reforms for women's rights. The indicators build evidence of the critical relationship between legal gender equality and women's employment and entrepreneurship.

By examining the economic decisions that women make throughout their working lives, as well as the progress made toward gender equality over the last 53 years, *Women, Business and the Law* continues to make important contributions to research and policy discussions about the state of women's economic empowerment. Data in *Women, Business and the Law 2023* are current as of October 1, 2022.

Boxes

Figures

Tables

FOREWORD

An economy is more dynamic, strong, and resilient when *all* citizens—women and men alike—can contribute equally. When laws restrict women's voice and agency, fail to protect them from violence, or discriminate them at the workplace and in retirement, women are less likely to participate fully in the economy and to contribute with their talent, knowledge, and skills. Economies that limit women's contributions cannot reach their full potential.

The World Bank's *Women, Business and the Law* project shows how equal legal rights and freedoms for women can be achieved around the world. It tracks how the law affects women's decisions and opportunities at various stages in their lives—from the essentials of freedom of movement and safety to the reconciliation of work and parenting, from the ability to own assets and access credit to the ability to inherit their fair share of property. It works under the premise—well supported by economic evidence—that a legal environment in which women have the same rights and opportunities as men leads to economic prosperity for everyone.

This year's *Women, Business and the Law* report brings some promising news. Last year, despite multiple overlapping global crises, most parts of the world strengthened legal gender equality across all areas measured. Economies in Sub-Saharan Africa led the way in 2022, enacting more than half of the reforms recorded. Many of these reforms addressed laws affecting women's pay and careers after having children—the areas with the most room to improve.

This year's report goes far beyond recent developments. It also provides the first comprehensive assessment of annual data gathered over more than five decades—from 1970 through 2022. Progress in this period has been remarkable: overall, economies have adopted more than 2,000 laws enhancing legal gender parity. The average *Women, Business and the Law* score has improved by about two-thirds as a result. Some of the strongest performers are economies that began with large gender-related legal gaps in the 1970s. The evidence is unmistakable: progress is possible when the right forces are at play.

Yet this good news is not nearly enough. The rate of progress has been uneven across economies, regions, and areas of reform. Only 14 economies have reached legal gender parity. The rate of catch-up has been slow. At today's pace, it will take several decades to close the legal gender gap across the world. This means that millions of young women entering the workforce today will have to wait until retirement—many even longer—before they get equal rights.

Today, nearly 2.4 billion working-age women live in economies that do not grant them the same rights as men. The year 2022 marks a low point in one respect: economies adopted the fewest gender-related reforms in more than two decades. In some economies, moreover, a troubling trend is under way: previously granted rights are being reversed. *Women, Business and the Law 2023* finds that some economies have made legal changes to strip women of existing rights, including the freedom of movement and the ability to get a job. Some have imposed additional burdens, like the duty of obedience to the husband. There is a lot to be done.

Empowering women is not just a matter of social justice. It is a prerequisite for economic development, especially at a time when global growth is slowing and economies will need to summon all of their productive energies to generate a lasting recovery from the crises of recent years. The World Bank Group is committed to help in instituting policies to ensure that women become full and equal participants in that recovery.

Indermit Gill
Chief Economist and Senior Vice President for Development Economics
World Bank Group

ACKNOWLEDGMENTS

Data collection and analysis for *Women, Business and the Law 2023* were conducted by a World Bank Group team led by Tea Trumbic (manager, *Women, Business and the Law*), under the general direction of Norman V. Loayza (director, Global Indicators Group, Development Economics). Overall guidance for preparation of the report was provided by Indermit Gill (chief economist and senior vice president, Development Economics) and Aart Kraay (deputy chief economist and director of development policy, Development Economics).

Members of the core research team were Nelsy Affoum, Nisha Arekapudi, Carolina Azcuña, Daniela Behr, Julia Constanze Braunmiller, Eduardo Calderón Pontaza, Mila Cantar, Alexis Koumjian Cheney, Claudia Lenny Corminales, Marie Dry, Rebecca Michelle Ego, Marina Elefante, Mahmoud Elsaman, Emilia Galiano, Bill Garthwaite, Mariam Anais Gnakra, Héloïse Groussard, Marie Caitriona Hyland, Viktoria Khaitina, Jungwon Kim, Shantel Marekera, Natália Mazoni Silva Martins, Olena Mykhalchenko, Hannelore Niesten, Caroline Perrin, Alena Sakhonchik, Isabel Santagostino Recavarren, Camelia Saranciuc, Liang Shen, Nayantara Vohra, Siyi Wang, Lara Wanna, and Yasmin Zand. The team was assisted by Consuelo Jurado Tan, Fahima Abdi Ali, Sakshi Chandra, Luiza Ferraz Di Ricco, Yoonhye Kim, Beryl Nana Ama Akuffo-Kwapong, Marla Munkh-Achit, Rosie Shrestha, Alisa Vithoontien, Yue (Sophie) Xi, and Yingxin Zhang.

Support for *Women, Business and the Law* is provided by the Bill & Melinda Gates Foundation; Childcare Incentive Fund; Human Rights, Inclusion and Empowerment Umbrella Trust Fund; Jobs Umbrella Multi-Donor Trust Fund; Knowledge for Change Program; State and Peacebuilding Fund; United States Agency for International Development; and William and Flora Hewlett Foundation.

The report was edited by Elizabeth Forsyth and Sabra Ledent and proofread by Catherine Farley. Dania Kibbi, Base Three Studio, was the principal graphic designer. Special thanks go to Stephen Pazdan, who coordinated and oversaw formal production of the report by the World Bank's publishing program. The team would also like to thank Jewel McFadden, who managed the overall publication process. The *Women, Business and the Law 2023* outreach strategy is managed by Joseph Rebello and supported by Shane Romig, Kristen Milhollin, Karolina Ordon, Mariana Lozzi Teixeira, and World Bank Group communications colleagues at headquarters and around the world. Development and management of the *Women, Business and the Law* website and other technical services are supported by Manasi Amalraj, Rajesh Ammassamveettil, Ying Chi, Varun Doiphode, Suman Gupta, Fengsheng Huang, Anna Maria Kojzar, Debora Manandhar, Akash Pradhan, Balasubramanian Ramakrishnan, Shrikant Bhaskar Shinde, and Geoffrey Shott. Shuting Sun and Divyanshi Wadhwa supported with data visualization. Monique Pelloux Patron and Van Thi Hong Do provided the team with resource management support. The team would also like to thank Irina Koval, Rose Gachina, and Tersit Berhane Ghiday for their help with coordination.

The team is grateful for valuable comments provided by Taylor Boyce, Nan Jiang, and other colleagues, both within and outside the World Bank Group, and for guidance provided by the World Bank Group's executive directors. The team would especially like to acknowledge the guidance of Brian Stacy, Divyanshi Wadhwa, Gero Carletto, Heather Moylan, Kathleen G. Beegle, and Umar Serajuddin. The team would also like to thank the many World Bank Group colleagues who provided written comments during the formal Bank-wide review process.

This report was made possible by the generous contributions of more than 2,400 lawyers, judges, academics, civil society representatives, and public officials from 190 economies. Contact details for local experts wishing to be acknowledged are available on the *Women, Business and the Law* website at https://wbl.worldbank.org. Firms that have completed multiple questionnaires from their various offices around the world are listed as global and regional contributors.

MAIN MESSAGES

Overview

Women, Business and the Law 2023 assesses laws and regulations on women's economic participation in 190 economies, from 1970 to 2022. The report covers eight related areas: Mobility, Workplace, Pay, Marriage, Parenthood, Entrepreneurship, Assets, and Pension. The data offer objective and measurable benchmarks for evaluating global progress toward legal gender equality.

Women, Business and the Law's analysis starts from the premise that gender equality is essential for ending extreme poverty and boosting shared prosperity. Equal treatment of women under the law is associated with larger numbers of women entering and remaining in the labor force and rising to managerial positions. It generates higher wages for women and facilitates more women owning a business.

Globally, on average, women enjoy only 77 percent of the legal rights that men do; and nearly 2.4 billion women of working age around the world live in economies that do not grant them the same rights as men. Although great achievements have been made in recent decades, much remains to be done (map 1).

Moreover, in 2022, the global pace of reforms toward equal treatment of women under the law has slumped to a 20-year low. This "reform fatigue" is a potential impediment to economic growth and resilience at a critical time for the global economy. As global economic growth is slowing, all countries need to mobilize their full productive capacity to confront the confluence of crises besetting them. Reforming in ways that encourage women to contribute to the economy as employees and entrepreneurs will both level the playing field and make the economy more dynamic and resilient in the face of shocks.

At the current pace of reform, it would take at least 50 years to approach legal gender equality everywhere. In many countries, a woman entering the workforce today will retire before gaining the same rights as men. In the areas measured in the report, it will take over 1,500 reforms to reach substantial legal gender equality around the world.

Gender-related reforms in 2022

In 2022, only 34 gender-related legal reforms were recorded across 18 economies—the lowest number since 2001. The global average score on the *Women, Business and the Law* index rose just half a point to 77.1 from 2021 to 2022. Most reforms focused on increasing paid leave for parents and fathers, removing restrictions on women's work, and mandating equal pay.

MAP 1 | THE GLOBAL AVERAGE *WOMEN, BUSINESS AND THE LAW* SCORE IS 77.1

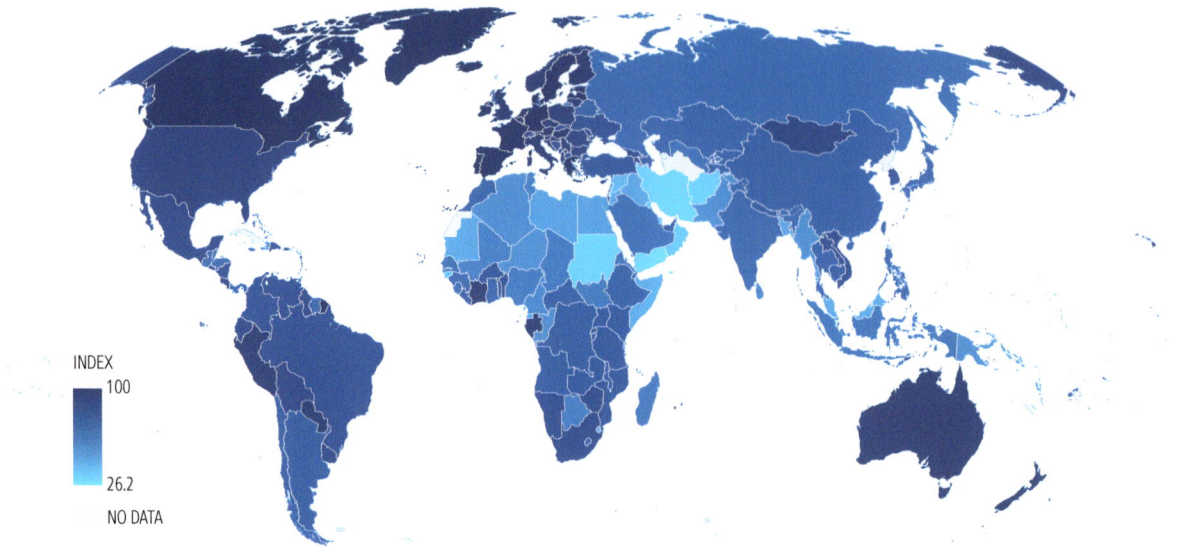

INDEX
100

26.2
NO DATA

IBRD 47032 | FEBRUARY 2023

Source: Women, Business and the Law database.

- Sub-Saharan Africa made significant progress last year. The region accounted for more than half of all reforms worldwide in 2022, with seven economies—Benin, the Republic of Congo, Côte d'Ivoire, Gabon, Malawi, Senegal, and Uganda—enacting 18 positive legal changes.

- In East Asia and Pacific, China introduced a parental leave policy, Indonesia enacted legislation protecting women from sexual harassment in employment, and Mongolia mandated equal remuneration for work of equal value and introduced paid paternity leave.

- The Middle East and North Africa also passed some significant reforms. Bahrain equalized the ages at which women and men can retire with full pension benefits. Iraq prohibited gender-based discrimination in financial services. Malta introduced paid parental leave for each parent.

- Economies in other regions also enacted reforms: Costa Rica, Jamaica, Kazakhstan, the Netherlands, and Pakistan.

Global progress toward gender equality in the last five decades

***Women, Business and the Law 2023* provides a comprehensive assessment of global progress toward gender equality in the law over the past five decades.** Spanning from 1970 to today, *Women, Business and the Law*'s historical database is an important tool for helping policy makers, civil society, the private sector, and researchers to understand the legal barriers facing women over time and around the world.

There is growing comparative evidence showing why countries decide to remove legal barriers for women. A country's institutional landscape, coupled with a stable economy and higher human capital, create the foundation for embarking on a reform process. The activism of women's groups and strategic multistakeholder coalitions help to create the momentum. Research and data are important tools for making the case for reforms. International legal mandates and technical assistance from international development partners offer key support for reformers seeking to identify good practices. These factors encourage and support the enactment of successful reforms.

Five main takeaways outline how, where, and how fast laws have changed since 1970:

1. Since 1970, the global average *Women, Business and the Law* score has improved by about two-thirds, rising from 45.8 to 77.1 points. The first decade of this century saw strong gains toward legal gender equality. Between 2000 and 2009, more than 600 reforms were introduced, with a peak of 73 reforms in 2002 and 2008. Since then, reform fatigue seems to have set in, particularly in areas that involve long-established norms, such as the rights of women to inherit and own property.

2. Today, just 14 economies—all high income—have laws giving women the same rights as men, and progress has been uneven across regions and over time. Worldwide, every economy has implemented at least one reform since 1970; however, 176 economies still have room to improve. Equality of economic opportunity for women is highest in Organisation for Economic Co-operation and Development (OECD) high-income economies, where the average score on the *Women, Business and the Law* index is 95.3 points, and lowest in the Middle East and North Africa region, where the average score is 53.2 points.

3. Progress across the areas measured has also been uneven, with most reforms in the areas of Workplace and Parenthood. Across all topic areas, most reforms have been issued to address domestic violence, prohibit gender discrimination in employment, and legislate on sexual harassment. The 1970s saw economies largely removing gender barriers on Mobility. The 1980s were characterized by isolated breakthroughs. The 1990s set the stage for a steep increase in women's legal empowerment, which picked up in the 2000s, a golden decade for women's legal rights in which economies reformed in all areas, with a remarkable spike in reforms under the Workplace indicator.

4. Economies with historically larger legal gender gaps have been catching up, especially since 2000. Faster progress is being made in economies that have had historically lower levels of gender equality. This is the case, for instance, in some countries in the Middle East and North Africa, and in Sub-Saharan Africa. Economies that have the highest growth rates in the *Women, Business and the Law* score include Bahrain, Botswana, the Democratic Republic of Congo, Indonesia, São Tomé and Príncipe, Saudi Arabia, South Africa, Togo, and the United Arab Emirates.

5. The catch-up effect has been happening across all areas covered by *Women, Business and the Law,* but the pace of progress has been uneven. The catch-up effect in closing the gender gap has been strongest in the laws affecting Workplace, followed by Parenthood, Pay, and Marriage. The catch-up effect has been weakest in laws related to Mobility, Assets, and Entrepreneurship.

Governments cannot afford to sideline as much as half of their population. Denying equal rights to women across much of the world not only is unfair to women, but also is a barrier to countries' ability to promote green, resilient, and inclusive development. Women cannot afford to wait any longer to reach gender equality. Neither can the global economy.

ABBREVIATIONS

BEE	Business Enabling Environment
COVID-19	coronavirus disease 2019
ES	Enterprise Survey
ILO	International Labour Organization
OECD	Organisation for Economic Co-operation and Development
SAR	Special Administrative Region
WBL	*Women, Business and the Law*

All dollar amounts are US dollars unless otherwise indicated.

Executive Summary

The state of women's legal rights

Policies empowering women strengthen the economy and are critical for lasting progress in development. Slowing global growth, the rising risks of climate change, conflict, and the lingering effects of COVID-19 have dealt a major setback to this progress in recent years—with disproportionate effects on the lives and livelihoods of women (Akrofi, Mahama, and Nevo 2021; De Paz, Gaddis, and Muller 2021; ILO 2022; Torres et al. 2021).

Women, Business and the Law's **analysis of 53 years of laws affecting women's economic rights shows why greater gender equality is essential for ending extreme poverty and boosting shared prosperity.** Equal treatment of women under the law is associated with larger numbers of women entering and remaining in the labor force and rising to managerial positions. It generates higher wages for women and facilitates more women owning a business.[1] Reforming in ways that incentivize women to enter the labor force—as employees and entrepreneurs—will both level the playing field and make the economy more robust in the face of shocks (Halim, O'Sullivan, and Sahay 2022; Ubfal 2022). *Women, Business and the Law* has tracked these regulatory changes from 1970 to today, offering objective benchmarks for measuring global progress toward gender equality in 190 economies.

Women, Business and the Law 2023 **details the current state of women's legal rights.** The ninth in a series, this study presents a data set and index structured around a woman's working life (figure ES.1) as well as findings from historical data that highlight opportunities for reform and can inspire efforts to seek equality. Governments, the private sector, and civil society can use this framework to identify and remove barriers to women's economic empowerment and boost labor force participation and

FIGURE ES.1 | EIGHT *WOMEN, BUSINESS AND THE LAW* INDICATORS MEASURE LEGAL DIFFERENCES BETWEEN MEN AND WOMEN AT DIFFERENT STAGES OF THEIR WORKING LIFE

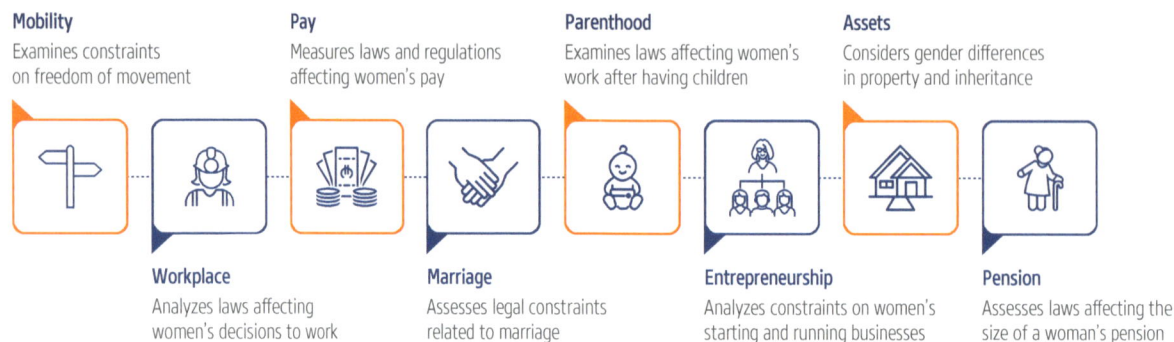

Mobility
Examines constraints on freedom of movement

Pay
Measures laws and regulations affecting women's pay

Parenthood
Examines laws affecting women's work after having children

Assets
Considers gender differences in property and inheritance

Workplace
Analyzes laws affecting women's decisions to work

Marriage
Assesses legal constraints related to marriage

Entrepreneurship
Analyzes constraints on women's starting and running businesses

Pension
Assesses laws affecting the size of a woman's pension

Source: Women, Business and the Law team.

entrepreneurship. The World Bank Group's lending and technical assistance operations use *Women, Business and the Law* data to provide the analytical underpinnings for project design. Other institutions—such as the Atlantic Council; Equal Measures 2030; the Georgetown Institute for Women, Peace and Security; the Heritage Foundation; the Millennium Challenge Corporation; and UN Women—use it to influence policy change.

Women still have only three-quarters of the legal rights of men, and nearly 2.4 billion women of working age still do not have the same legal rights as men. The global average *Women, Business and the Law* score is 77.1 out of 100 in 2022, only half a point higher than in 2021. Today, 14 economies (Belgium, Canada, Denmark, France, Germany, Greece, Iceland, Ireland, Latvia, Luxembourg, the Netherlands, Portugal, Spain, and Sweden) score 100 on the index, meaning that women are on an equal legal standing with men in all of the areas measured (table ES.1). Nearly 90 million women of working age gained legal equality in the last decade. Yet, 2.4 billion women of working age do not have the same legal rights as men. More than half live in East Asia and Pacific (710 million) and South Asia (610 million), followed by Sub-Saharan Africa (330 million), Organisation for Economic Co-operation and Development (OECD) high income (260 million), Latin America and the Caribbean (210 million), Middle East and North Africa (150 million), and Europe and Central Asia (140 million). Economies with average scores above the global average of 77.1 tend to be in OECD high income, Europe and Central Asia, and Latin America and the Caribbean regions (figure ES.2). The Middle East and North Africa as well as South Asia have the lowest average scores.

Progress toward equal treatment for women has fallen to its weakest pace in 20 years. Since 2021, 18 economies introduced a total of 34 reforms toward gender equality across all areas measured by *Women, Business and the Law* (figure ES.3), the lowest number since 2001. Sub-Saharan Africa accounts for more than half of all reforms, with seven economies—Benin, the Republic of Congo, Côte d'Ivoire, Gabon, Malawi, Senegal, and Uganda—enacting 18 positive legal changes. Among these, two economies stand out: Côte d'Ivoire and Gabon. Côte d'Ivoire enacted reforms prohibiting discrimination in access to credit based on gender, addressing domestic violence, and removing restrictions on women's employment. Gabon continued along the path of reform undertaken last year, equalizing the process for obtaining a passport, mandating

FIGURE ES.2 | THE LARGEST GAPS ARE IN THE MIDDLE EAST AND NORTH AFRICA AND IN SUB-SAHARAN AFRICA

Dispersion of Women, Business and the Law 2023 *average scores, by region*

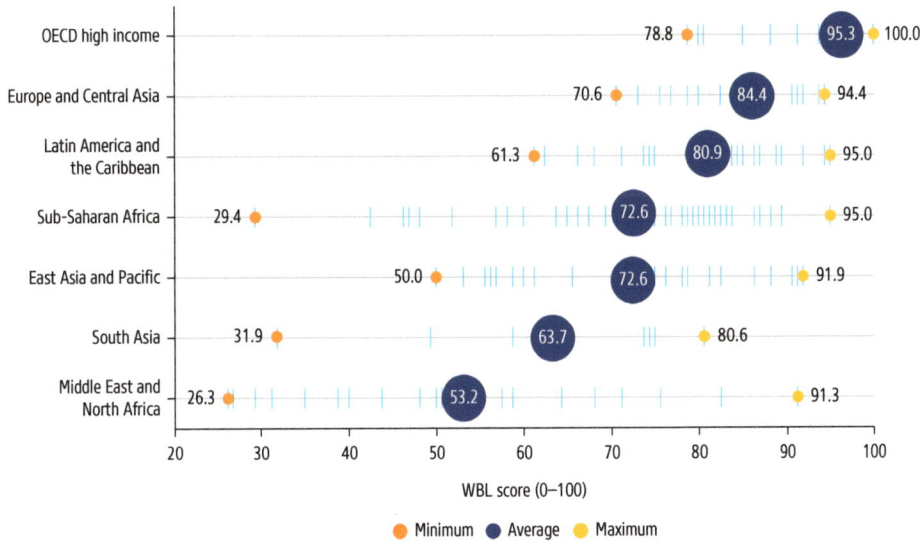

Source: Women, Business and the Law database.
Note: Each vertical line represents the score of an economy in its respective region. Each blue circle indicates the average score for a region. The minimum and maximum scores within each region are specified. OECD = Organisation for Economic Co-operation and Development.

FIGURE ES.3 | IN 2021–22, 18 ECONOMIES ENACTED REFORMS ACROSS ALL *WOMEN, BUSINESS AND THE LAW* INDICATORS

Count of reforms since October 2021, by economy, indicator, and region

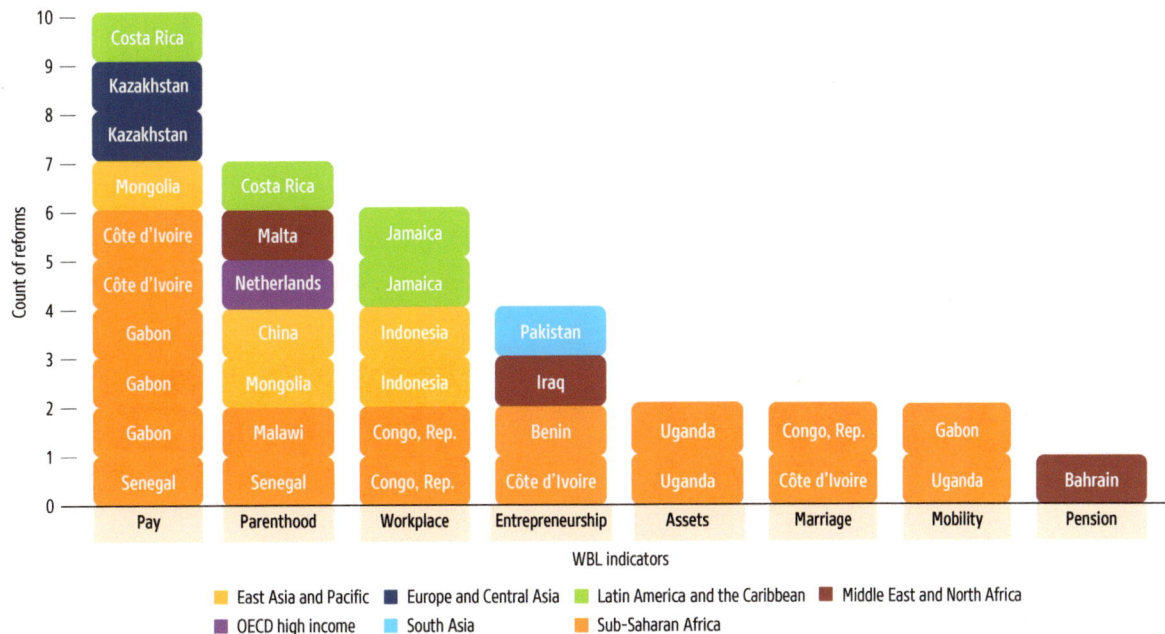

Source: Women, Business and the Law database.
Note: OECD = Organisation for Economic Co-operation and Development.

TABLE ES.1		EIGHTEEN ECONOMIES IMPROVED THEIR *WOMEN, BUSINESS AND THE LAW 2023* SCORE							
Economy	Score	Economy	Score	Economy	Score	Economy	Score	Economy	Score
Belgium	100.0	Malta ✓	91.3	St. Lucia	83.8	Burundi	76.3	Botswana	63.8
Canada	100.0	Taiwan, China	91.3	São Tomé and Príncipe	83.1	Kiribati	76.3	Mali *	63.8
Denmark	100.0	United States	91.3	Burkina Faso	82.5	Seychelles	76.3	Dominica	62.5
France	100.0	Bulgaria	90.6	Fiji	82.5	Belarus	75.6	Haiti	61.3
Germany *	100.0	Mongolia ✓	90.6	Mozambique	82.5	Kazakhstan ✓	75.6	Micronesia, Fed. Sts.	61.3
Greece	100.0	Romania	90.6	Singapore	82.5	Morocco	75.6	Cameroon	60.0
Iceland	100.0	Ecuador	89.4	Türkiye	82.5	Bhutan *	75.0	Papua New Guinea	60.0
Ireland	100.0	Mauritius	89.4	United Arab Emirates	82.5	Ghana	75.0	Lebanon	58.8
Latvia	100.0	Bolivia	88.8	Togo	81.9	Honduras	75.0	Myanmar	58.8
Luxembourg	100.0	El Salvador	88.8	Bahamas, The	81.3	Samoa	75.0	Pakistan ✓	58.8
Netherlands ✓	100.0	Mexico	88.8	Cambodia	81.3	Trinidad and Tobago	75.0	Tonga	58.8
Portugal	100.0	Uruguay	88.8	Liberia	81.3	India	74.4	Congo, Rep. ✓	58.1
Spain	100.0	Georgia	88.1	Tanzania	81.3	Jamaica ✓	74.4	Algeria	57.5
Sweden	100.0	Lao PDR	88.1	Uganda ✓	81.3	Guatemala *	73.8	Niger	56.9
Estonia	97.5	South Africa	88.1	Zambia	81.3	Guinea	73.8	Solomon Islands	56.9
Finland	97.5	Switzerland	88.1	Grenada	80.6	Maldives	73.8	Palau	56.3
Italy	97.5	Vietnam *	88.1	Israel	80.6	Suriname	73.8	Vanuatu	55.6
New Zealand	97.5	Armenia	87.5	Kenya	80.6	Russian Federation	73.1	Brunei Darussalam	53.1
United Kingdom	97.5	Moldova	87.5	Nepal	80.6	Senegal ✓	72.5	Equatorial Guinea	51.9
Australia	96.9	Guyana	86.9	Barbados	80.0	Sierra Leone	72.5	Egypt, Arab Rep.	50.6
Austria	96.9	Zimbabwe	86.9	Chile	80.0	Djibouti *	71.3	Libya	50.0
Hungary	96.9	Cabo Verde	86.3	Malawi ✓	80.0	Saudi Arabia ✗	71.3	Malaysia	50.0
Norway	96.9	Dominican Republic	86.3	San Marino	80.0	St. Kitts and Nevis	71.3	Bangladesh	49.4
Slovenia	96.9	Namibia	86.3	Angola	79.4	Indonesia ✓	70.6	Iraq ✓	48.1
Côte d'Ivoire ✓	95.0	Nicaragua	86.3	Argentina	79.4	Uzbekistan	70.6	Mauritania	48.1
Gabon ✓	95.0	Timor-Leste	86.3	Belize	79.4	Eritrea	69.4	Jordan	46.9
Peru	95.0	Bosnia and Herzegovina	85.0	Panama	79.4	Gambia, The	69.4	Somalia	46.9
Cyprus	94.4	Brazil	85.0	Azerbaijan	78.8	Madagascar *	69.4	Eswatini	46.3
Paraguay	94.4	Korea, Rep.	85.0	Congo, Dem. Rep.	78.8	Bahrain ✓	68.1	Guinea-Bissau	42.5
Croatia	93.8	Montenegro	85.0	Japan	78.8	St. Vincent and the Grenadines	68.1	Syrian Arab Republic	40.0
Czechia	93.8	North Macedonia	85.0	Philippines	78.8	South Sudan	67.5	Oman	38.8
Lithuania	93.8	Slovak Republic	85.0	Tajikistan	78.8	Antigua and Barbuda	66.3	Kuwait	35.0
Poland	93.8	Ukraine	85.0	China ✓	78.1	Chad	66.3	Afghanistan ✗	31.9
Serbia	93.8	Venezuela, RB	85.0	Lesotho	78.1	Nigeria *	66.3	Iran, Islamic Rep.	31.3
Costa Rica ✓	91.9	Colombia	84.4	Thailand	78.1	Marshall Islands	65.6	Qatar	29.4
Hong Kong SAR, China	91.9	Benin ✓	83.8	Central African Republic	76.9	Sri Lanka	65.6	Sudan	29.4
Kosovo	91.9	Puerto Rico (US)	83.8	Ethiopia	76.9	Comoros	65.0	Yemen, Rep.	26.9
Albania	91.3	Rwanda	83.8	Kyrgyz Republic	76.9	Tunisia	64.4	West Bank and Gaza	26.3

Source: Women, Business and the Law database.

Note: Economies with a green check (✓) saw an improvement in score due to reforms in one or more areas. Economies with a red X (✗) introduced at least one legal change that reduced the score. Economies with an asterisk (*) saw a change in their score due to revisions made as a result of new information (Djibouti, Germany, Guatemala, Vietnam) and coding consistency (Bhutan, Madagascar, Mali, Nigeria).

equal remuneration for work of equal value, and removing all job restrictions for women. As a result, for the first time in 53 years, two economies from the Sub-Saharan Africa region score above 90 on the *Women, Business and the Law* index, and the average score for the Sub-Saharan Africa region has surpassed the score of the East Asia and Pacific region. Other countries that reformed this year are Bahrain, China, Costa Rica, Indonesia, Iraq, Jamaica, Kazakhstan, Malta, Mongolia, the Netherlands, and Pakistan.

Most reforms focused on increasing paid leave for parents and fathers, removing restrictions on women's work, and mandating equal pay. Although the Parenthood and Pay indicators have the most room to improve, with average scores of 56.4 and 70.0, respectively, they also registered the most reforms in 2022. Seven economies in five regions reformed laws measured by the Parenthood indicator. Specifically, China, Malta, and the Netherlands mandated paid parental leave, Costa Rica, Malawi, and Mongolia introduced paid paternity leave, and Senegal amended its law to prohibit the dismissal of pregnant women. Additionally, six economies in four regions enacted reforms captured by the Pay indicator. Costa Rica, Côte d'Ivoire, Gabon, Kazakhstan, and Senegal removed restrictions on women's work. Gabon and Mongolia also introduced provisions mandating equal remuneration for work of equal value.

Data trends from five decades of reform

The *Women, Business and the Law* historical data highlight the benefits of reform. Spanning from 1970 to today, *Women, Business and the Law*'s historical database is an important tool for understanding the geographic and chronological dimensions of legal barriers faced by women. Removing legal constraints for women has been shown to be associated with various metrics of women's economic opportunity and socioeconomic development. The ability to act autonomously and work without legal limitations also allows women to access better jobs and can lead to higher labor force participation overall (Amin and Islam 2015; Htun, Jensenius, and Nelson-Nuñez 2019). Moreover, freedom from discrimination helps women to become entrepreneurs and access finance (Islam, Muzi, and Amin 2019). Evidence is also growing that family leave policies are correlated with women's empowerment. For example, Amin and Islam (2022) find a significant positive association between the legislated number of maternity leave days and female employment at the firm level. Evidence is emerging that gender equality is important not just for women's economic empowerment but also for macroeconomic development. Recent studies show that removing legal barriers for women can help poorer economies to catch up with richer economies (Sever 2022). This growing body of evidence highlights the need to continue working to level the legal playing field between women and men.

Comparative evidence is also growing to show why countries decide to remove legal barriers for women. For example, a common driver for the expansion of women's rights is the evolution of a country's political system. The extent to which various groups can participate in the decision-making institutions of a democratic economy matters, as does a civil society that is actively challenging societal order or mobilizing action. Education and higher human capital are also important enablers for the expansion of women's rights. Tertilt et al. (2022) show that economic development is an important predictor of women's rights. Case studies of historical legal reforms aimed at gender equality in the Democratic Republic of Congo, Ethiopia, India, Kenya, São Tomé and

Príncipe, South Africa, Togo, and the United Arab Emirates reveal that international legal mandates, technical assistance from international development partners, the activism of women's groups, strategic multistakeholder coalitions, and the use of research and data are all decisive factors encouraging and supporting the enactment of successful reforms. Efforts to shed more light on what factors are driving reforms can guide future policy and expedite movement toward legal gender equality. They are a crucial first step toward identifying key challenges and opportunities to accelerate women's economic empowerment around the world.

Five main takeaways outline how, where, and how fast laws have changed since 1970. To provide more legal rights for women, economies have reformed existing laws or introduced new legislation. By tracking these changes, *Women, Business and the Law* highlights the remarkable catch-up effect in some economies. The findings underscore that reform efforts are happening around the world, irrespective of income level, culture, or region.

1. **In the last five decades, the global average of the *Women, Business and the Law* score has improved by about two-thirds as a result of more than 2,000 reforms expanding women's legal rights.** Over the course of 53 years, economies have introduced an impressive 2,151 reforms in all 35 areas of measurement, increasing the global average *Women, Business and the Law* score from 45.8 to 77.1 points. Between 2000 and 2009, more than 600 reforms were introduced, with a peak of 73 annual reforms in 2002 and 2008. However, since then, the pace of reform has slowed, and economies seem to be exhibiting reform fatigue in addressing notoriously stickier areas of the law such as Mobility and Assets. For instance, reforming inheritance laws will inevitably challenge long-established norms, and legislative measures might be slow and incremental. In 2022, only 34 reforms were recorded, a historic low since 2001. It will take another 1,549 reforms to reach legal gender equality everywhere.

2. **Only 14 economies have achieved legal gender parity in 2022, as measured by *Women, Business and the Law,* and progress has been uneven across regions and over time.** Worldwide, every economy has implemented at least one reform since 1970, allowing women to move one step closer to gender parity under the law. Despite this progress, gender disparities persist in all regions and all income levels: 176 economies still have room to improve, and at the recent pace of reform they will need at least another 50 years to reach 100.[2] This means that a young woman entering the workforce today will retire before she is able to enjoy gender equal rights during her working life. Yet given the rather slow progress in some areas, such as reforming laws related to inheritance rights, it may take many more years to close existing gender gaps across all areas. Today, equality of economic opportunity for women is highest in OECD high-income economies, where the average score on the *Women, Business and the Law* index is 95.3 points, and lowest in the Middle East and North Africa region, where the average score is 53.2 points. There are also regional differences in the timing of reform efforts. Economies in Latin America and the Caribbean reformed substantially in the 1990s. Sub-Saharan Africa saw a significant spike in reforms in the 2000s, with the adoption of the Protocol to the African Charter on Human and Peoples' Rights on the Rights of Women in Africa (the Maputo Protocol). The Middle East and North Africa's reform efforts did not take off until the 2010s (figure ES.4);

FIGURE ES.4 | PROGRESS TOWARD GENDER-EQUAL LAWS HAS BEEN UNEVEN ACROSS TIME AND REGIONS

Number of women's rights reforms implemented, by decade and region

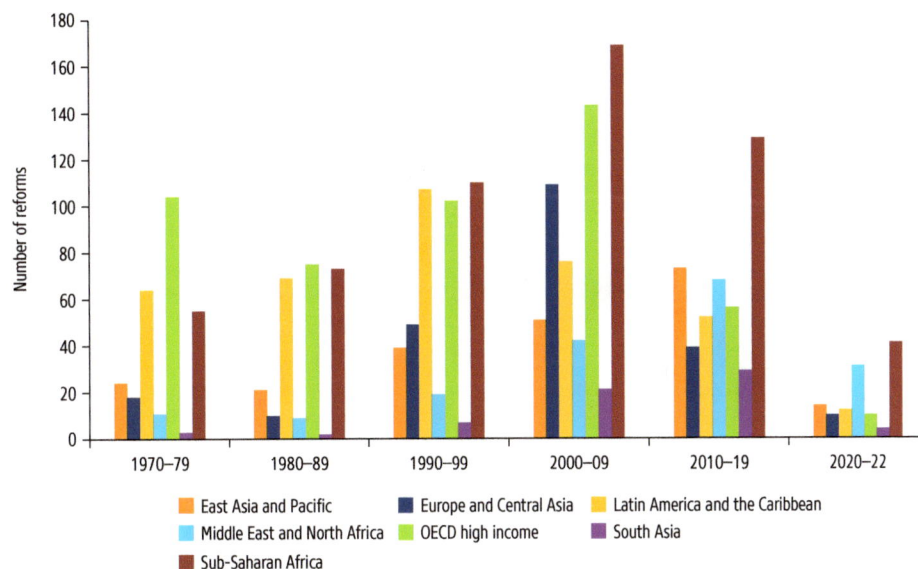

Source: Women, Business and the Law database.
Note: The figure shows the number of reforms, by region, that removed legal gender barriers. A reform is counted if, within any of the 35 areas of measurement, an answer changes from "no" to "yes" because of the adoption of a new law or the amendment of an existing law. The last set of bars reflects reforms enacted in only three years: 2020, 2021, and 2022. All regions are classified as of 2022. OECD = Organisation for Economic Co-operation and Development.

since then, the region has implemented more reforms (100) than in the previous four decades combined (81 reforms from 1970 to 2009). The differences in reform efforts have been less pronounced across income groups.

3. **Progress across the areas measured has also been uneven, with most reforms in Workplace and Parenthood**. Across all topic areas, most reforms have been issued to address domestic violence, prohibit gender discrimination in employment, and legislate on sexual harassment. Reform efforts have unfolded in waves, with a focus on specific areas. In the 1970s, economies largely removed gender barriers on mobility, allowing married women to choose where to live, and introduced legislation addressing the dismissal of pregnant workers. In some instances, the removal of restrictions on women's mobility was due to the overhaul of legacy civil codes that had been in place during colonial times. In other cases, archaic national legislation dating back to the previous century was finally updated. The 1980s was a decade of isolated breakthroughs, but the 1990s set the stage for a steep increase in women's legal empowerment: 19 economies mandated equal remuneration for work of equal value, 10 granted women at least 14 weeks of paid maternity leave, and 38 introduced domestic violence legislation. The 2000s were a golden decade for women's legal rights: economies reformed in all areas, with a remarkable spike in reforms under the Workplace indicator.

4. **Economies with historically larger legal gender gaps have been catching up, especially since 2000.** Analysis of the annual growth rate in the *Women, Business and the Law* index shows that faster progress is being made in economies that have had a historically lower level of gender equality. The two economies that have had the fastest annual growth rates in the index are São Tomé and Príncipe and the United Arab Emirates. While reform in São Tomé and Príncipe has been a gradual process since 1970, with some intermediary periods where the pace of reform slowed and then, after a time, gathered pace again, reforms in the United Arab Emirates took off only in recent years. Other economies that are among the fastest reformers, with annualized growth rates in the index in the top fifth percentile, are Bahrain, Botswana, the Democratic Republic of Congo, Indonesia, Saudi Arabia, South Africa, and Togo.

5. **The catch-up effect has been happening across all areas covered by *Women, Business and the Law*, but the pace of progress has been uneven.** The catch-up effect has been strongest in the laws affecting women's decisions to enter and remain in the labor force, followed by those affecting women's work after the birth of a child, and the right to receive equal pay (figure ES.5). The catch-up effect has been weakest in laws related to agency and freedom of movement, and property and inheritance rights.

FIGURE ES.5 | HISTORICALLY MORE UNEQUAL AREAS HAVE REFORMED FASTER OVER TIME

Evolution of Women, Business and the Law *indicator scores, 1970–2022*

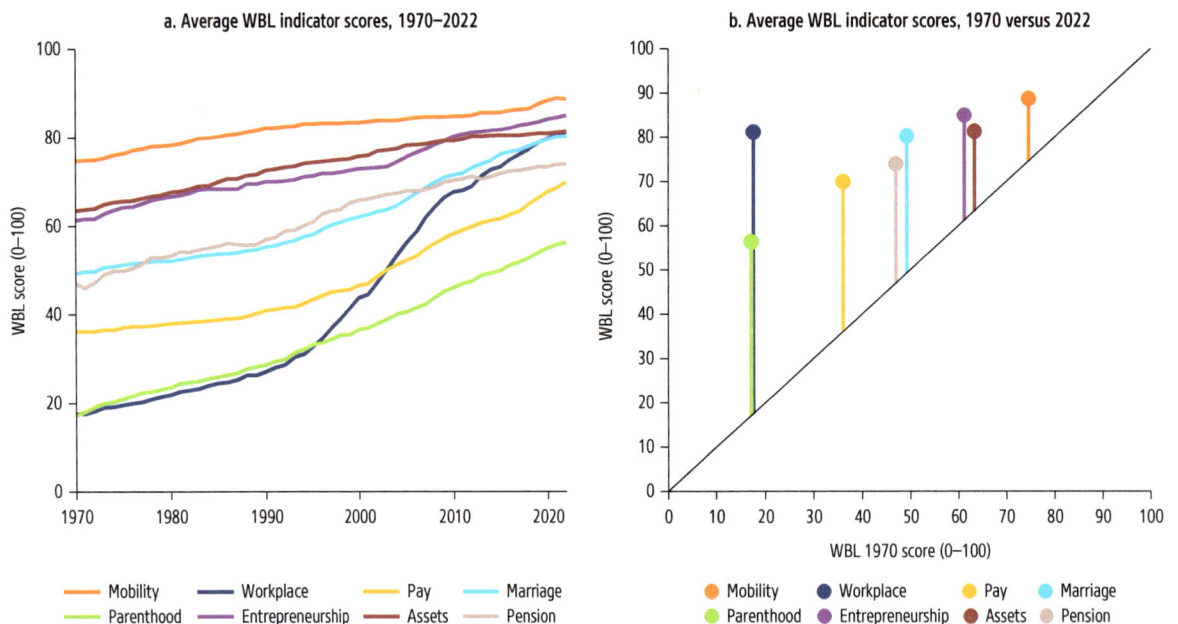

Source: Women, Business and the Law database.

Overcoming legal gender barriers benefits all of society—not just women. Although reform efforts are happening around the world, appalling gaps in women's rights persist today in all regions, especially in the areas of leave policies and equal pay. Ninety-three economies still do not mandate equal remuneration for work of equal value, and some economies are even reversing rights for which women have fought long and hard. Nevertheless, women worldwide remain important agents of change in demanding their equal rights and opportunities, even under dire circumstances. Policy makers should reinforce these efforts because overcoming legal gender barriers benefits the economy as a whole, not just women. The *Women, Business and the Law* data present a unique opportunity to assess countries' performances in closing legal gender gaps and to inspire policy makers to remove existing discriminatory laws. Although great achievements have been made over the last five decades, more and better data are needed, and more needs to be done worldwide to ensure that good intentions are accompanied by tangible results—that is, equal opportunity under the law for women. In an era when economies everywhere will need to mobilize every ounce of productive capacity to generate sufficient growth, sidelining half the population constitutes an egregious waste. Women cannot afford to wait another 50 years or more to reach equality. Neither can the global economy.

What's next

Women, Business and the Law **continues to expand its substantial research agenda.** Recognizing the formidable challenges facing women, *Women, Business and the Law* is exploring several areas of research aimed at expanding the reach of the indicators (figure ES.6). Building on evidence and preliminary data collected and analyzed over the last several years, *Women, Business and the Law 2024* will publish data on new indicators measuring childcare legislation and implementation of the law. The team is also expanding data and analysis on measures related to women's safety and embarking on a review of areas in which legal equality has almost been reached, such as the right of women to sign a contract in the same way as men, a right now granted by 99 percent of economies. This pilot data set will be published in *Women, Business and the Law 2024* and fully integrated into the index and report in the 2025 edition.

FIGURE ES.6 | **EXPANDING THE SCOPE OF THE *WOMEN, BUSINESS AND THE LAW* INDEX**

WBL **2023**	WBL **2024**	WBL **2025**
Research on childcare, implementation, safety, and other areas	Publication of new data on childcare, disability, implementation, and safety	Incorporation of new indicators into WBL index and report

Source: Women, Business and the Law team.

Notes

1. This research includes Amin and Islam (2015); Htun, Jensenius, and Nelson-Nuñez (2019); and Islam, Muzi, and Amin (2019), all of which use cross-country data from the *Women, Business and the Law* project, as well as country-specific studies such as Zabalza and Tzannatos (1985). Roy (2019) provides an overview of the evidence linking legal gender equality and women's economic outcomes.
2. If all economies reform equally across all indicators, at the pace seen in the past year, it will take at least another 50 years to reach 100.

References

Akrofi, Mark M., Mudasiru Mahama, and Chinedu M. Nevo. 2021. "Nexus between the Gendered Socio-economic Impacts of COVID-19 and Climate Change: Implications for Pandemic Recovery." *SN Social Sciences* 1 (8): 198. doi:10.1007/s43545-021-00207-5.

Amin, Mohammad, and Asif M. Islam. 2015. "Does Mandating Nondiscrimination in Hiring Practices Influence Women's Employment? Evidence Using Firm-Level Data." *Feminist Economics* 21 (4): 28–60.

Amin, Mohammad, and Asif M. Islam. 2022. "The Impact of Paid Maternity Leave on Women's Employment." Policy Research Working Paper 10188, World Bank, Washington, DC.

De Paz, Nieven Carmen, Isis Gaddis, and Miriam Muller. 2021. "Gender and COVID-19: What Have We Learnt, One Year Later." Policy Research Working Paper 9709, World Bank, Washington, DC.

Halim, Daniel, Michael B. O'Sullivan, and Abhilasha Sahay. 2022. "Thematic Policy Brief on Increasing Female Labor Force Participation." World Bank, Washington, DC.

Htun, Mala, Francesca Jensenius, and Jami Nelson-Nuñez. 2019. "Gender-Discriminatory Laws and Women's Economic Agency." *Social Politics: International Studies in Gender, State, and Society* 26 (2): 193–222. doi:10.1093/sp/jxy042.

ILO (International Labour Organization). 2022. *World Employment and Social Outlook: Trends 2022*. Geneva: ILO.

Islam, Asif, Silvia Muzi, and Mohammad Amin. 2019. "Unequal Laws and the Disempowerment of Women in the Labour Market: Evidence from Firm-Level Data." *Journal of Development Studies* 55 (5): 822–44. doi:10.1080/00220388.2018.1487055.

Roy, Sanchari. 2019. "Discriminatory Laws against Women: A Survey of the Literature." Policy Research Working Paper 8719, World Bank, Washington, DC.

Sever, Can. 2022. "Legal Gender Equality as a Catalyst for Convergence." IMF Working Paper WP/22/155, International Monetary Fund, Washington, DC.

Tertilt, Michèle, Matthias Doepke, Anne Hannusch, and Laura Montenburck. 2022. "The Economics of Women's Rights." NBER Working Paper 30617, National Bureau of Economic Research, Cambridge, MA.

Torres, Jesica, Franklin Maduko, Isis Gaddis, Leonardo Iacovone, and Kathleen Beegle. 2021. "The Impact of the COVID-19 Pandemic on Women-Led Businesses." Policy Research Working Paper 9817, World Bank, Washington, DC.

Ubfal, Diego. 2022. "What Works in Supporting Women-Led Businesses?" Thematic Policy Brief for Gender Strategy Update, World Bank, Washington, DC.

Zabalza, Antoni, and Zafiris Tzannatos. 1985. "The Effect of Britain's Anti-Discriminatory Legislation on Relative Pay and Employment." *Economic Journal* 95 (379): 679–99. doi:10.2307/2233033.

CHAPTER 1

The State of Women's Legal Rights

Introduction

After decades of subjugation to her husband's will, in 2021 a woman in South Africa challenged his marital power in court and won (Arekapudi and Mazoni 2022). In Costa Rica in 2022, the female president of the Legislative Assembly successfully ensured that a woman could freely pursue a job of her choice, eliminating archaic prohibitions on the types of work a woman can perform (Sequeira 2022). In Côte d'Ivoire, the work of national government agencies tasked with consolidating the rights of women led to the adoption of the country's first law on domestic violence and legislation enabling women's employment and entrepreneurship.

These women's successes are recent, and yet they build on the accomplishments of those who have tirelessly worked to remove the legal barriers that hinder women's full enjoyment of rights and opportunities. Their stories are powerful examples of the elements that make change possible, illustrating lessons learned and proving that achieving gender equality takes a concerted effort by persons from all corners of society.

Women, Business and the Law has tracked regulatory changes in some of the areas key to women's economic empowerment from 1970 to today, offering objective and measurable benchmarks for global progress toward gender equality in 190 economies. Gender equality is essential to end extreme poverty and boost shared prosperity. Yet discriminatory laws persist in all regions, threatening not only women's human rights, but also their ability to participate meaningfully in the global economy. In 2010 no woman in the world had the same legal rights to economic opportunity as men in the areas measured by *Women, Business and the Law*. Between 2010 and 2022, this situation changed, as more than 93 million women of working age (15–64) gained the same legal rights as men in the areas measured (figure 1.1). However, the progress is

FIGURE 1.1 | MORE THAN 90 MILLION WOMEN OF WORKING AGE HAVE GAINED LEGAL EQUALITY IN THE LAST DECADE

Number of working-age women with the same legal rights as men, 2010–21

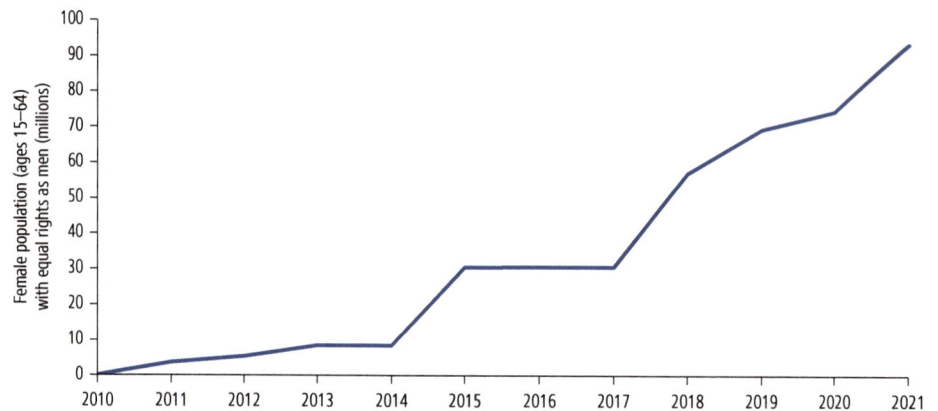

Sources: Women, Business and the Law database and World Development Indicators database.

not fast enough, as worldwide across all regions, nearly 2.4 billion women of working age still do not have the same legal rights as men. More than half of these women live in East Asia and Pacific (710 million) and South Asia (610 million), followed by Sub-Saharan Africa (330 million), Organisation for Economic Co-operation and Development (OECD) high income (260 million), Latin America and the Caribbean (210 million), Middle East and North Africa (150 million), and Europe and Central Asia (140 million).

Women, Business and the Law 2023 identifies where and in what areas of study this inequality prevails, providing an important resource for achieving women's economic empowerment. The ninth in a series, this study presents a data set and index that highlight opportunities for reform and findings from historical data that can inspire current and future efforts to seek equality.

For nearly 15 years, *Women, Business and the Law* has served as a framework that governments and civil society alike can use to identify and remove barriers to women's success and boost labor force participation. Since 2020, an index structured around a woman's working life has guided the analysis, celebrating the progress made while emphasizing the work still to be done (box 1.1).

The findings are an important tool for use in policy discussions about the state of women's empowerment and overall economic resilience. Indeed, research undertaken by the *Women, Business and the Law* team reveals that more equal laws are associated with more women working, higher wages, more women-owned businesses, and more women in managerial positions.[1] With evidence mounting of these positive effects, gender equality needs to become an international priority. This development is especially relevant in view of the pressing challenges that continue to confront the global economy (World Bank 2023). The threat of a global recession, climate crisis, conflict, and the lingering effects of COVID-19 not only threaten economic resilience, but also disproportionately affect women's lives and livelihoods (Akrofi, Mahama, and Nevo 2021; De Paz, Gaddis, and Muller 2021; ILO 2022; Torres et al. 2021).

BOX 1.1 ABOUT *WOMEN, BUSINESS AND THE LAW*

***Women, Business and the Law* identifies laws that restrict women's economic inclusion.** Its index aligns different areas of the law with the economic decisions that women make throughout their lives and careers (figure B1.1.1).

FIGURE B1.1.1 | THE EIGHT *WOMEN, BUSINESS AND THE LAW* INDICATORS

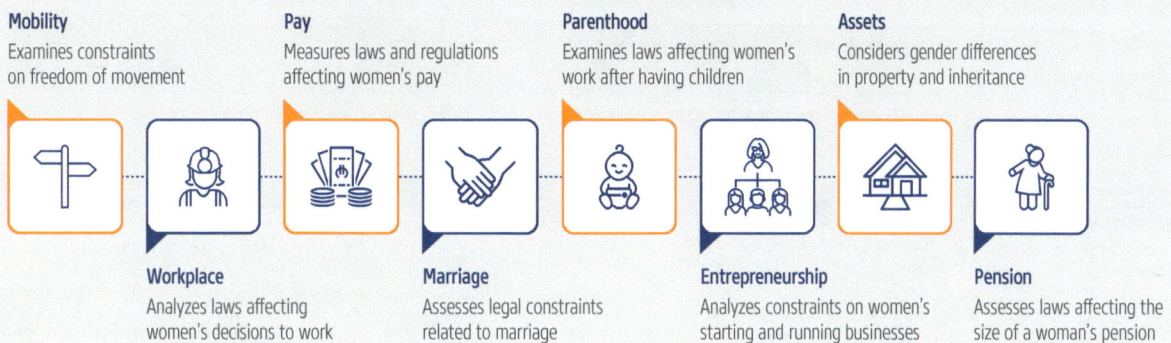

Mobility
Examines constraints on freedom of movement

Pay
Measures laws and regulations affecting women's pay

Parenthood
Examines laws affecting women's work after having children

Assets
Considers gender differences in property and inheritance

Workplace
Analyzes laws affecting women's decisions to work

Marriage
Assesses legal constraints related to marriage

Entrepreneurship
Analyzes constraints on women's starting and running businesses

Pension
Assesses laws affecting the size of a woman's pension

Source: Women, Business and the Law team.

The eight *Women, Business and the Law* indicators coincide with milestones that many women experience and reflect the international legal framework. The questions under each indicator were chosen based on evidence from the economic literature and statistically significant associations with outcomes related to women's economic empowerment, such as employment and business ownership. The international legal framework on women's human rights, as set out in the Convention on the Elimination of All Forms of Discrimination against Women (CEDAW) and International Labour Organization conventions, also provides underlying justification for each question. The indicators measure explicit discrimination in the law as well as the legal protection of rights and provision of benefits—areas in which reforms can bolster women's economic participation.

In total, 35 questions are scored across the eight indicators. Indicator-level scores are obtained by calculating the simple average of the four or five binary questions within that indicator and scaling the result to 100. Overall scores are then calculated by taking the average of each indicator, with 100 representing the highest possible score and indicating equal rights and opportunities for men and women in all 35 areas of measurement (see the data notes in appendix A for details). This score can be interpreted as the absence of legal inequality for a woman throughout her working life. Although other rights not part of the *Women, Business and the Law* data set are certainly also important, these 35 areas constitute a foundational set of rights essential for equal economic opportunities between women and men throughout their working lives. The final score summarizes good-practice legal provisions on gender parity in each economy. Thus, the index serves as a gauge of the enabling environment for women as entrepreneurs and employees.

The *Women, Business and the Law* index relies on a series of assumptions. This approach has both strengths and limitations (table B1.1.1). For example, the woman in question is assumed to reside in the main business city of her economy and to be employed in the formal sector. This approach may not capture restrictions applicable to areas outside the main business city or to informal workers. However, four of the eight indicators have direct relevance for women who work in the informal sector— for example, laws affecting women's freedom of movement, their ability to own or inherit property, or protections against domestic violence. Additionally, legal protections affecting the formal sector provide a foundation for economic inclusion and offer incentives for women to be employed in or start businesses in the formal sector and to transition from the informal to the formal economy. Still, the interplay of other factors, such as access to quality education, infrastructural and institutional capacity, and social and cultural norms may prevent women from entering the workforce. This study recognizes these limitations. Although they may come at the expense of specificity, they also ensure that the data are reliable and comparable.

(Box continues next page)

BOX 1.1 ABOUT *WOMEN, BUSINESS AND THE LAW (continued)*

TABLE B1.1.1	METHODOLOGICAL STRENGTHS AND LIMITATIONS OF THE *WOMEN, BUSINESS AND THE LAW* INDEX	
Feature	**Strength**	**Limitation**
Use of standardized assumptions	Data are comparable across economies, and methodology is transparent.	The scope of data is smaller; only regulatory reforms in the areas measured can be tracked systematically.
Coverage of largest business city only	Data collection is manageable, and data are comparable.	In federal economies, data may be less representative where laws differ across locations.
Focus on the most populous group	Data are comparable across economies where parallel legal systems prescribe different rights for different groups of women.	Restrictions that apply to minority populations may not be captured.
Emphasis on the formal sector	Attention remains centered on the formal economy, where regulations are most relevant.	The reality faced by women in the informal sector, which may be a significant population in some economies, is not fully reflected.
Measure of codified laws only	Indicators are actionable because the law is what policy makers can change.	Where systematic implementation of legislation is lacking, regulatory changes alone will not achieve the desired results; social and cultural norms are not considered.

Source: *Women, Business and the Law* database.

To construct the index, *Women, Business and the Law* surveys more than 2,000 experts in family, labor, and violence against women legislation. Questionnaire respondents include lawyers, judges, academics, and members of civil society organizations working locally on gender issues. Although many legal experts contribute over consecutive report cycles, the base of respondents has been expanded over time to include new voices and contributions. *Women, Business and the Law* collects the texts of relevant laws and regulations and verifies responses to questionnaires for accuracy. Responses are validated against codified sources of national law in areas such as labor, social security, civil procedure, violence against women, marriage and family, inheritance, nationality, and land. All of the data used to construct the index are available on the *Women, Business and the Law* website (https://wbl.worldbank.org).

Reforming in ways that incentivize women to enter the labor force as employees and entrepreneurs will both level the playing field and make the economy more robust in the face of shocks (Halim, O'Sullivan, and Sahay 2022; Ubfal 2022) (box 1.2). While progress has been made over the last 53 years, at the current pace of legal reform it will take at least another 50 years for economies to reach equality in the areas measured. *Women, Business and the Law* will continue to explore these challenges and the critical relationship between economic outcomes and to build the case for gender equality in all areas of life.

Data update

Women, Business and the Law 2023 updates its index to account for legal reforms that took place from October 2, 2021, to October 1, 2022. During that period, the global average score rose about half a point over the previous cycle, reaching 77.1 out of 100. Five years ago, the global average score was 73.8. Women in just 14 of 190 economies have the same legal rights as men in all of the indicators measured: Belgium, Canada, Denmark, France, Germany, Greece, Iceland, Ireland, Latvia, Luxembourg, the Netherlands, Portugal, Spain, and Sweden (table 1.1). For the complete *Women, Business and the Law* data set, see the economy data in appendix B.

BOX 1.2 HOW *WOMEN, BUSINESS AND THE LAW* DATA AND FINDINGS CAN BE USED TO PROMOTE POLICY REFORM

Women, Business and the Law research and data can provide important evidence to inform the design of policy interventions that promote women's economic empowerment. Increasingly, the World Bank Group's lending and technical assistance operations are using *Women, Business and the Law* data to provide the analytical underpinnings for project design. In 2019, the World Bank's Investing in Human Capital Development Policy Financing supported the government of Madagascar's ambitious agenda to improve human capital, including by strengthening legal frameworks for the protection of women and girls. *Women, Business and the Law* data helped to identify critical legislative gaps, such as lack of legal protection against domestic violence, leading to the adoption of the country's first violence against women legislation. The following year, the Lifting Legal Barriers to Women's Employment in Azerbaijan project provided technical assistance to the government of Azerbaijan and led to the adoption of labor reforms removing job restrictions for women identified by *Women, Business and the Law* data. In 2021, *Women, Business and the Law* data informed the design of Benin's Unlocking Human and Productive Potential Development Policy Operation and helped to identify key legal gender gaps in the area of gender-based violence. In Sierra Leone, the 2022 Inclusive and Sustainable Growth Development Policy Operation used *Women, Business and the Law* data to advance reforms prohibiting sex-based discrimination in the provision of financial services.

Women, Business and the Law data are also used by other institutions to influence policy change. For example, together with UN Women and the Organisation for Economic Co-operation and Development, *Women, Business and the Law* contributes its data and expertise to inform Sustainable Development Goal 5.1.1 (https://unstats.un.org/sdgs/metadata/): "Whether or not legal frameworks are in place to promote, enforce, and monitor equality and non-discrimination on the basis of sex." The Millennium Challenge Corporation (https://www.mcc.gov/who-we-select/indicator/gender-in-the-economy-indicator) uses *Women, Business and the Law* data in its Gender in the Economy indicator, which is used to assess economies' commitments to promoting gender equality. Several other institutions use *Women, Business and the Law* data to construct their own indexes, such as the Georgetown Institute for Women, Peace, and Security's index (https://giwps.georgetown.edu/the-index/), the Heritage Foundation's Index of Economic Freedom (https://www.heritage.org/index/), the Atlantic Council's Freedom and Prosperity Indexes (https://www.atlanticcouncil.org/programs/freedom-and-prosperity-center/), the International Trade Center's SheTrades Outlook (https://intracen.org/resources/tools/shetrades-outlook), the Equal Measures 2030's SDG Gender Index (https://www.equalmeasures2030.org/2022-sdg-gender-index/), and the Global Governance Forum's Gender Equality and Governance Index (GEGI) (https://globalgovernanceforum.org/global-issues/gender-equality/), among others. Arizona State University's Global SDG 5 Notification Tool (https://globalfutures.asu.edu/sdg5-training/) also provides users with insight into country-level progress on legal gender equality and aims to inform parliamentarians about the status of their laws ahead of the United Nations Human Rights Council's Universal Periodic Review for their country.

These are just a few examples of how different stakeholders can use *Women, Business and the Law* data to achieve the same goal—removing discriminatory laws that hinder women's economic inclusion and promoting good-practice legislation that incentivizes women's economic participation.

Globally, 44 economies in six regions score above 90. Among them, 28 are in OECD high income, 7 are in Europe and Central Asia, 3 are in East Asia and Pacific, and 3 are in Latin America and the Caribbean. In 2022, 1 economy in the Middle East and North Africa region (Malta) and 2 economies in the Sub-Saharan Africa region (Côte d'Ivoire and Gabon) also score above 90 for the first time. No economy in the South Asia region has reached a score of 90.

Economies in the low- and middle-income groups made significant progress toward legal gender equality in the past year. Seven lower-middle-income economies implemented 15 reforms, leading to an increase of 0.8 points in average score. Upper-middle-income economies also improved their average score by 0.8 points with 12 reforms. Low-income economies followed with an increase of 0.2 points, reaching an overall score of 66.3, after enacting four reforms. Although the average score of

TABLE 1.1		WOMEN, BUSINESS AND THE LAW 2023 SCORE							
Economy	Score	Economy	Score	Economy	Score	Economy	Score	Economy	Score
Belgium	100.0	Malta ✓	91.3	St. Lucia	83.8	Burundi	76.3	Botswana	63.8
Canada	100.0	Taiwan, China	91.3	São Tomé and Príncipe	83.1	Kiribati	76.3	Mali *	63.8
Denmark	100.0	United States	91.3	Burkina Faso	82.5	Seychelles	76.3	Dominica	62.5
France	100.0	Bulgaria	90.6	Fiji	82.5	Belarus	75.6	Haiti	61.3
Germany *	100.0	Mongolia ✓	90.6	Mozambique	82.5	Kazakhstan ✓	75.6	Micronesia, Fed. Sts.	61.3
Greece	100.0	Romania	90.6	Singapore	82.5	Morocco	75.6	Cameroon	60.0
Iceland	100.0	Ecuador	89.4	Türkiye	82.5	Bhutan *	75.0	Papua New Guinea	60.0
Ireland	100.0	Mauritius	89.4	United Arab Emirates	82.5	Ghana	75.0	Lebanon	58.8
Latvia	100.0	Bolivia	88.8	Togo	81.9	Honduras	75.0	Myanmar	58.8
Luxembourg	100.0	El Salvador	88.8	Bahamas, The	81.3	Samoa	75.0	Pakistan ✓	58.8
Netherlands ✓	100.0	Mexico	88.8	Cambodia	81.3	Trinidad and Tobago	75.0	Tonga	58.8
Portugal	100.0	Uruguay	88.8	Liberia	81.3	India	74.4	Congo, Rep. ✓	58.1
Spain	100.0	Georgia	88.1	Tanzania	81.3	Jamaica ✓	74.4	Algeria	57.5
Sweden	100.0	Lao PDR	88.1	Uganda ✓	81.3	Guatemala *	73.8	Niger	56.9
Estonia	97.5	South Africa	88.1	Zambia	81.3	Guinea	73.8	Solomon Islands	56.9
Finland	97.5	Switzerland	88.1	Grenada	80.6	Maldives	73.8	Palau	56.3
Italy	97.5	Vietnam *	88.1	Israel	80.6	Suriname	73.8	Vanuatu	55.6
New Zealand	97.5	Armenia	87.5	Kenya	80.6	Russian Federation	73.1	Brunei Darussalam	53.1
United Kingdom	97.5	Moldova	87.5	Nepal	80.6	Senegal ✓	72.5	Equatorial Guinea	51.9
Australia	96.9	Guyana	86.9	Barbados	80.0	Sierra Leone	72.5	Egypt, Arab Rep.	50.6
Austria	96.9	Zimbabwe	86.9	Chile	80.0	Djibouti *	71.3	Libya	50.0
Hungary	96.9	Cabo Verde	86.3	Malawi ✓	80.0	Saudi Arabia ✗	71.3	Malaysia	50.0
Norway	96.9	Dominican Republic	86.3	San Marino	80.0	St. Kitts and Nevis	71.3	Bangladesh	49.4
Slovenia	96.9	Namibia	86.3	Angola	79.4	Indonesia ✓	70.6	Iraq ✓	48.1
Côte d'Ivoire ✓	95.0	Nicaragua	86.3	Argentina	79.4	Uzbekistan	70.6	Mauritania	48.1
Gabon ✓	95.0	Timor-Leste	86.3	Belize	79.4	Eritrea	69.4	Jordan	46.9
Peru	95.0	Bosnia and Herzegovina	85.0	Panama	79.4	Gambia, The	69.4	Somalia	46.9
Cyprus	94.4	Brazil	85.0	Azerbaijan	78.8	Madagascar *	69.4	Eswatini	46.3
Paraguay	94.4	Korea, Rep.	85.0	Congo, Dem. Rep.	78.8	Bahrain ✓	68.1	Guinea-Bissau	42.5
Croatia	93.8	Montenegro	85.0	Japan	78.8	St. Vincent and the Grenadines	68.1	Syrian Arab Republic	40.0
Czechia	93.8	North Macedonia	85.0	Philippines	78.8	South Sudan	67.5	Oman	38.8
Lithuania	93.8	Slovak Republic	85.0	Tajikistan	78.8	Antigua and Barbuda	66.3	Kuwait	35.0
Poland	93.8	Ukraine	85.0	China ✓	78.1	Chad	66.3	Afghanistan ✗	31.9
Serbia	93.8	Venezuela, RB	85.0	Lesotho	78.1	Nigeria *	66.3	Iran, Islamic Rep.	31.3
Costa Rica ✓	91.9	Colombia	84.4	Thailand	78.1	Marshall Islands	65.6	Qatar	29.4
Hong Kong SAR, China	91.9	Benin ✓	83.8	Central African Republic	76.9	Sri Lanka	65.6	Sudan	29.4
Kosovo	91.9	Puerto Rico (US)	83.8	Ethiopia	76.9	Comoros	65.0	Yemen, Rep.	26.9
Albania	91.3	Rwanda	83.8	Kyrgyz Republic	76.9	Tunisia	64.4	West Bank and Gaza	26.3

Source: Women, Business and the Law database.

Note: Economies with a green check (✓) saw an improvement in score due to reforms in one or more areas. Economies with a red X (✗) introduced at least one legal change that reduced the score. Economies with an asterisk (*) saw a change in their score due to revisions made as a result of new information (Djibouti, Germany, Guatemala, Vietnam) and coding consistency (Bhutan, Madagascar, Mali, Nigeria).

high-income economies is 86.9, some economies in this group still have scores as low as 29.4. In fact, in all income groups gaps of at least 48 points are evident between the lowest- and highest-scoring economies, indicating that women still face significant differences in their legal standing even in places at similar levels of economic development (figure 1.2). Many factors drive differences in scores within the same income level. For example, conflict and fragility can contribute to lack of reforms toward gender equality. Violent conflicts and high levels of institutional and social fragility affect the quality of policy and institutions, including government capacity to undertake reforms. Out of 27 low-income economies examined, 11 economies with the lowest *Women, Business and the Law* scores are also fragile and conflict-affected situations, consisting of Afghanistan, Chad, Eritrea, Guinea-Bissau, Mali, Niger, Somalia, South Sudan, Sudan, the Syrian Arab Republic, and the Republic of Yemen.

The state of women's legal equality varies within and among regions. Regions with average scores higher than the global average of 77.1 are OECD high income, Europe and Central Asia, and Latin America and the Caribbean. The Middle East and North Africa and South Asia remain the two regions with the lowest average scores (figure 1.3). The gap between the lowest-scoring and highest-scoring economies in Sub-Saharan Africa and the Middle East and North Africa is close to 65 points. Economies in these regions can learn from their neighbors or inspire others to reform.

Thanks to reforms in Sub-Saharan Africa, this year the pattern among regions has changed for the first time since 2004. This year, Sub-Saharan Africa surpassed the

FIGURE 1.2 | **SCORE GAPS OF MORE THAN 50 POINTS EXIST ACROSS ALL INCOME GROUPS**

Dispersion of Women, Business and the Law *average scores, by income level*

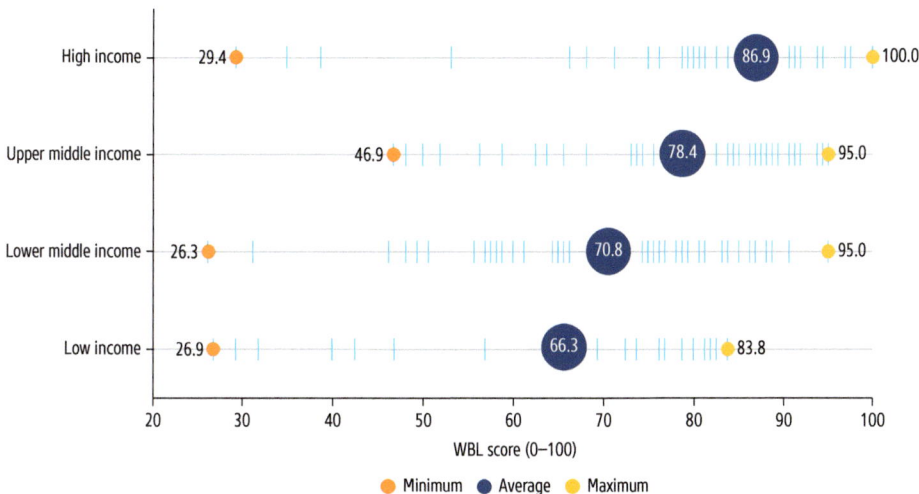

Source: Women, Business and the Law database.

Note: Each vertical line represents the score of an economy in its respective income group. Each blue circle indicates the average score for an income group. The minimum and maximum scores within each group are specified. All income groups are classified as of 2022, except for República Bolivariana de Venezuela, which is included in the upper-middle-income group, as last classified in 2021.

FIGURE 1.3 | **THE LARGEST GAPS ARE IN THE MIDDLE EAST AND NORTH AFRICA AND IN SUB-SAHARAN AFRICA**

Dispersion of Women, Business and the Law 2023 *average scores, by region*

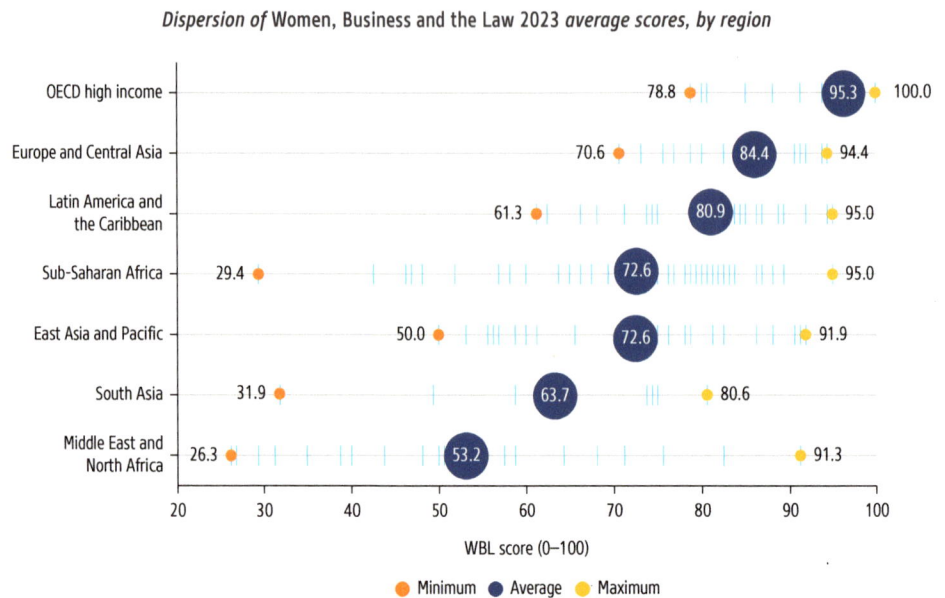

Source: Women, Business and the Law database.
Note: Each vertical line represents the score of an economy in its respective region. Each blue circle indicates the average score for a region. The minimum and maximum scores within each region are specified. OECD = Organisation for Economic Co-operation and Development.

average score of East Asia and Pacific for the first time in the past 53 years (figure 1.4, panel a). OECD high-income economies continue to have the highest average scores, followed by Europe and Central Asia and Latin America and the Caribbean. The region that advanced the most due to reform efforts is the Middle East and North Africa, the lowest scoring region, with an increase of over 9 points in its overall score over the last five years. Economies in Sub-Saharan Africa and South Asia, with scores below the global average, have increased their score by more than 4 points since 2017, substantially improving legal equality for women (figure 1.4, panel b).

Seven of the eight indicators improved in score over the past year (annex 1B). For Mobility, legal changes widening the gender gap resulted in a decrease of 0.1 points. This year, apart from Parenthood (56.4), Pay (70.0), and Pension (73.9), all other indicators score 80 or above on average. The Pay indicator has the second-to-lowest average score, and it increased by 1.3 points—the largest improvement among all indicators. This is followed by an increase of 0.7 points in Parenthood and Workplace, respectively, and 0.5 points in Entrepreneurship. The indicator sequence has not changed substantively, with Mobility, Entrepreneurship, and Assets still having the highest scores and Pay and Parenthood having the lowest scores today as well as five years ago (figure 1.5, panel a). Despite lower scores, however, indicators that improved the most are Pay and Workplace, both with an increase of at least 5 points over the last five years (figure 1.5, panel b). Parenthood's score also has increased by 4.5 points since 2017, indicating improved legal equality for women after they have children.

FIGURE 1.4 | OVER THE LAST FIVE YEARS, REGIONS SCORING THE LOWEST IMPROVED THE MOST

Improvements in Women, Business and the Law *scores, 2018–23, by region*

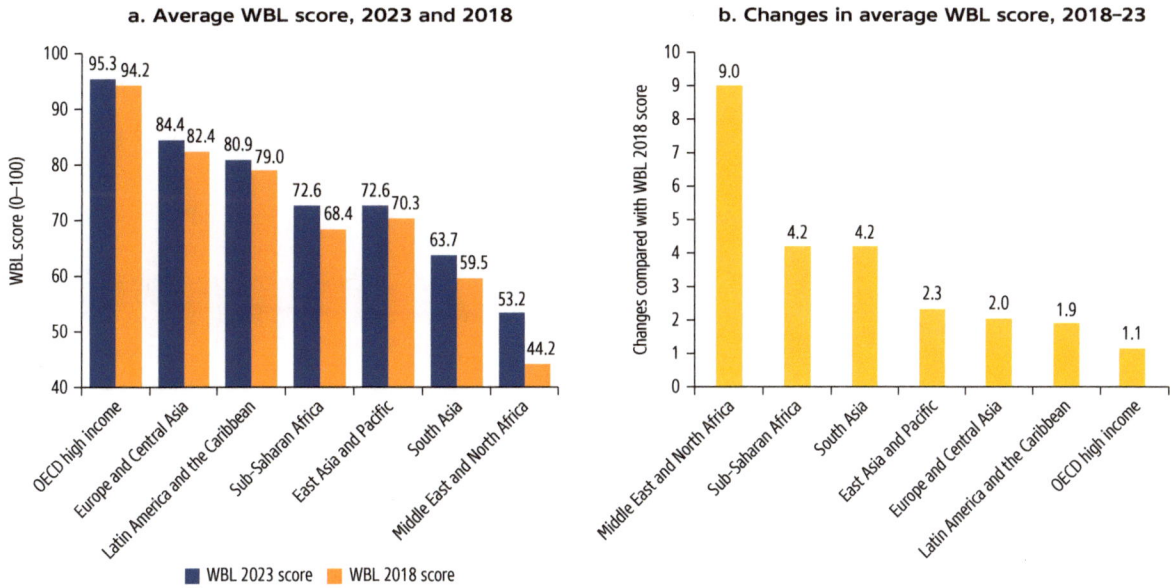

a. Average WBL score, 2023 and 2018

b. Changes in average WBL score, 2018–23

■ WBL 2023 score ■ WBL 2018 score

Source: Women, Business and the Law *database.*
Note: OECD = Organisation for Economic Co-operation and Development.

FIGURE 1.5 | DESPITE IMPROVEMENTS IN THE PAST FIVE YEARS, PAY AND PARENTHOOD STILL HAVE THE LOWEST SCORES

Improvements in Women, Business and the Law *scores, 2018–23, by indicator*

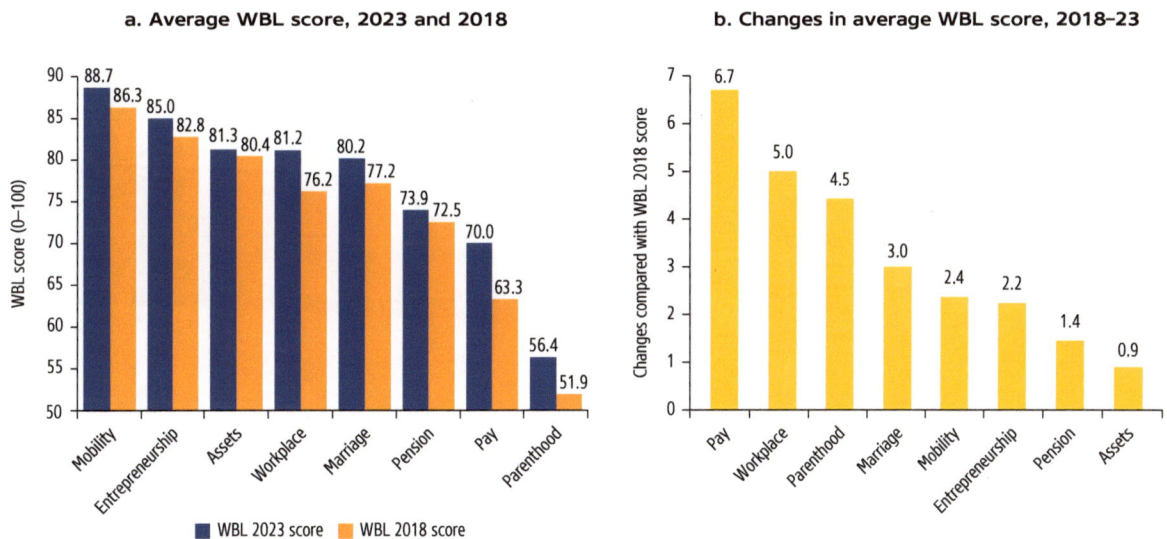

a. Average WBL score, 2023 and 2018

b. Changes in average WBL score, 2018–23

■ WBL 2023 score ■ WBL 2018 score

Source: Women, Business and the Law *database.*

Where are laws changing?

In the past year, 18 economies in all regions introduced 34 reforms across all indicators to accelerate progress toward achieving legal gender equality (table 1.2).

Seven economies in Sub-Saharan Africa—Benin, the Republic of Congo, Côte d'Ivoire, Gabon, Malawi, Senegal, and Uganda—implemented 18 positive reforms (box 1.3). The region accounts for more than half of all reforms in the past year (figure 1.6, panel a). The International Labour Organization (ILO) estimates suggest that in Sub-Saharan Africa, 90 percent of working women are employed informally compared to 83 percent of men (ILO 2022), meaning that they are employed in work that does not provide legal protections. In Côte d'Ivoire alone, more than 80 percent of women are employed in nonagricultural work in the informal sector compared with 60 percent of men. This means that the impact of some of the reforms, including Workplace, Pay, Parenthood, and Pension, and the reality faced by women in the informal sector may not always be fully reflected. Informality is an important factor in understanding the distinction between legal changes on paper and their application in practice. However, reforms in Mobility, Marriage, Entrepreneurship, and Assets apply to women regardless of their official employment.

Three economies in the East Asia and Pacific region—China, Indonesia, and Mongolia—also enacted five positive legal changes. Despite the region's relatively high average score, two economies in Latin America and the Caribbean implemented four changes boosting gender equality: Costa Rica and Jamaica. Three reforms were

TABLE 1.2	IN 2021–22, ECONOMIES IMPLEMENTED THE HIGHEST NUMBER OF REFORMS TO IMPROVE GENDER EQUALITY IN THE PAY INDICATOR		
Indicator	Number of reforms	Economies	Details of reforms
Mobility	2	Gabon, Uganda	Gabon enacted legislation allowing women to apply for a passport in the same way as men.
			Uganda granted women the same rights to choose where to live as men.
Workplace	6	Congo, Rep.; Indonesia; Jamaica	The Republic of Congo, Indonesia, and Jamaica enacted legislation on sexual harassment in employment, including criminal penalties and civil remedies.
Pay	10	Costa Rica, Côte d'Ivoire, Gabon, Kazakhstan, Mongolia, Senegal	Costa Rica, Côte d'Ivoire, Gabon, Kazakhstan, and Senegal eliminated various types of restrictions on women's employment.
			Mongolia and Gabon mandated equal remuneration for work of equal value.
Marriage	2	Congo, Rep.; Côte d'Ivoire	The Republic of Congo and Côte d'Ivoire enacted legislation protecting women from various forms of domestic violence.
Parenthood	7	China, Costa Rica, Malawi, Malta, Mongolia, the Netherlands, Senegal	China, Malta, and the Netherlands introduced paid parental leave.
			Costa Rica, Malawi, and Mongolia introduced paid paternity leave.
			Senegal prohibited the dismissal of pregnant workers.
Entrepreneurship	4	Benin, Côte d'Ivoire, Iraq, Pakistan	Benin, Côte d'Ivoire, and Iraq prohibited discrimination based on gender in access to credit.
			Pakistan allowed women to register a business in the same way as men.
Assets	2	Uganda	Uganda equalized inheritance rights for spouses and between sons and daughters.
Pension	1	Bahrain	Bahrain equalized the ages at which men and women can retire with full pension benefits.

Source: Women, Business and the Law database.
Note: "Number of reforms" refers to data points that changed because of the reform implemented. For the full list of reforms, see annex 1B.

BOX 1.3 SPOTLIGHT ON SUB-SAHARAN AFRICA

Women, Business and the Law has observed a rise in reform activity in Sub-Saharan Africa since October 2021, leading to a 1.1-point increase in the region's average score. Eighteen positive reforms were implemented by seven economies— Benin, the Republic of Congo, Côte d'Ivoire, Gabon, Malawi, Senegal, and Uganda—accounting for more than half of all reforms captured. Although from the same region, these economies are relatively diverse: two are low income (Malawi and Uganda), four are lower middle income (Benin, the Republic of Congo, Côte d'Ivoire, and Senegal), and one is upper middle income (Gabon). Progress is also occurring widely across the whole region, with reforms captured in West, Central, East, and southern Africa and across all indicators, with the exception of Pension.

Côte d'Ivoire and Gabon have had impressive reform agendas, becoming the first two economies in Sub-Saharan Africa with scores of at least 90. Both economies embarked on substantial revisions of legislation affecting women's **pay.** Côte d'Ivoire's Decree No. 2021-919 removed all existing restrictions on the employment of women in certain types of jobs and industries, whether dangerous, arduous, or morally inappropriate. Similarly, Gabon's 2021 amendments to its labor code removed restrictions on women's ability to engage in hazardous and arduous work. Furthermore, the amendments mandate for the first time that for work of equal value, equal remuneration should be provided for all workers regardless of their origin, opinion, sex, or age. Senegal also reformed in this area, removing restrictions on women working in industrial jobs.

The Republic of Congo and Côte d'Ivoire also made remarkable strides in addressing **gender-based violence against women.** Specifically, both economies adopted laws addressing domestic violence for the first time. Both laws address all forms of domestic violence, including physical, sexual, psychological, and economic forms of abuse, with criminal penalties and special procedures to obtain protection orders against perpetrators. The Republic of Congo also criminalized sexual harassment in employment, with penalties ranging from a fine to imprisonment of up to 10 years.

Benin and Côte d'Ivoire promoted women's **financial inclusion** by prohibiting gender-based discrimination in financial services. Benin's 2022 Order No. 2349-5 prohibits credit institutions, banking-type financial institutions, and decentralized financial systems from discriminating based on gender in access to credit. Côte d'Ivoire's Law No. 2021-893 amends the criminal code to sanction sex-based discrimination in the provision of goods, credit, and services with a fine and imprisonment of up to three years.

Change in the region is also occurring in areas harder to reform because of inherent costs, such as **paid family leave,** or social norms, such as **mobility and inheritance.** In Malawi in 2021, amendments to the Employment Act entitled fathers to at least two weeks of paternity leave with full pay. Senegal amended its Labor Code and prohibited the dismissal of pregnant women. Gabon and Uganda removed important restrictions on women's mobility. By eliminating the requirement for married women to obtain marital authorization when applying for a passport, Gabon made it easier for women to travel abroad. Uganda's 2022 Succession (Amendment) Act also removed an existing requirement for women to acquire their husbands' domicile upon marriage by adopting gender-neutral language that now allows a woman to choose where to live in the same way as a man. Remarkably, the same act also amended previous provisions that favored sons over daughters in inheritance and denied widows any entitlements to the matrimonial home and other property, redefining a legal heir to include females and guaranteeing equal distribution of the property of an intestate. The law was passed after years of delay to update antiquated provisions and finally addressed a notoriously difficult area of reform.

Although the sequencing of reforms in these economies has varied based on the specific country context, the changes in the region demonstrate that both targeted and comprehensive reforms are possible with the right conditions and motivations. As this pattern of steady reform demonstrates, holistic reform efforts can lead to a considerably more favorable legal environment for working women in Sub-Saharan Africa.

FIGURE 1.6 | SUB-SAHARAN AFRICAN AND LOWER-MIDDLE-INCOME ECONOMIES REFORMED THE MOST

Reforms, by region and income group

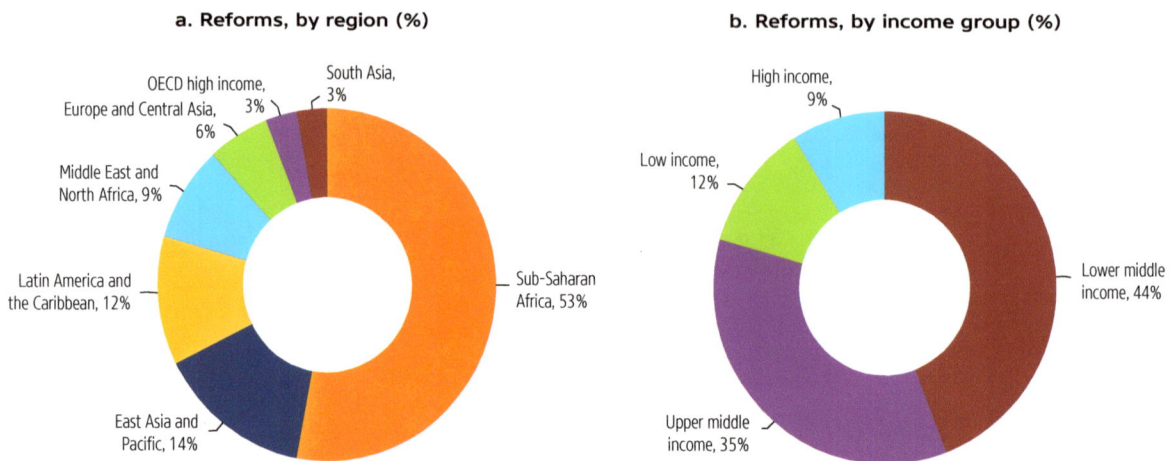

a. Reforms, by region (%)

OECD high income, 3%
Europe and Central Asia, 6%
South Asia, 3%
Middle East and North Africa, 9%
Latin America and the Caribbean, 12%
East Asia and Pacific, 14%
Sub-Saharan Africa, 53%

b. Reforms, by income group (%)

High income, 9%
Low income, 12%
Lower middle income, 44%
Upper middle income, 35%

Source: Women, Business and the Law database.
Note: OECD = Organisation for Economic Co-operation and Development.

implemented in the Middle East and North Africa: one each in Bahrain, Iraq, and Malta. The remaining reforms were in Kazakhstan in Europe and Central Asia, the Netherlands among the OECD high-income economies, and Pakistan in South Asia.

Among the economies that implemented at least one reform that improved legal equality for women, lower-middle-income economies account for close to 45 percent, upper-middle-income economies for more than 35 percent, and low-income economies for more than 10 percent (figure 1.6, panel b). High-income economies account for the smallest share of all reforms (9 percent), but these economies already had the highest scores. Among the economies in Sub-Saharan Africa that improved laws on gender equality, Côte d'Ivoire stands out for having implemented four reforms in three areas: Entrepreneurship, Marriage, and Pay. More specifically, it enacted laws that prohibit discrimination in access to credit based on gender and that address domestic violence and include physical, sexual, and psychological abuse. Côte d'Ivoire also no longer restricts women's employment in certain types of jobs and industries. As a result of these reforms, Côte d'Ivoire increased its score by almost 12 points (from 83.1 to 95.0) and became one of the first two countries in Sub-Saharan Africa to score at least 90. The other country is Gabon, which continued down the reform path it launched last year by equalizing the process for obtaining passports, mandating equal remuneration for work of equal value, and removing all job restrictions for women.

Most positive reforms in 2022 were within the Parenthood and Pay indicators (figure 1.7). These indicators also have the most room to improve. Seven economies in five regions implemented changes to laws as measured by the Parenthood indicator. Specifically, three economies (China, Malta, and the Netherlands) mandated paid parental leave, three economies (Costa Rica, Malawi, and Mongolia) introduced paternity leave for fathers, and one economy (Senegal) amended its law to prohibit the dismissal of pregnant women.

FIGURE 1.7 | IN 2021–22, 18 ECONOMIES ENACTED REFORMS ACROSS ALL *WOMEN, BUSINESS AND THE LAW* INDICATORS

Count of reforms since October 2021, by economy, indicator, and region

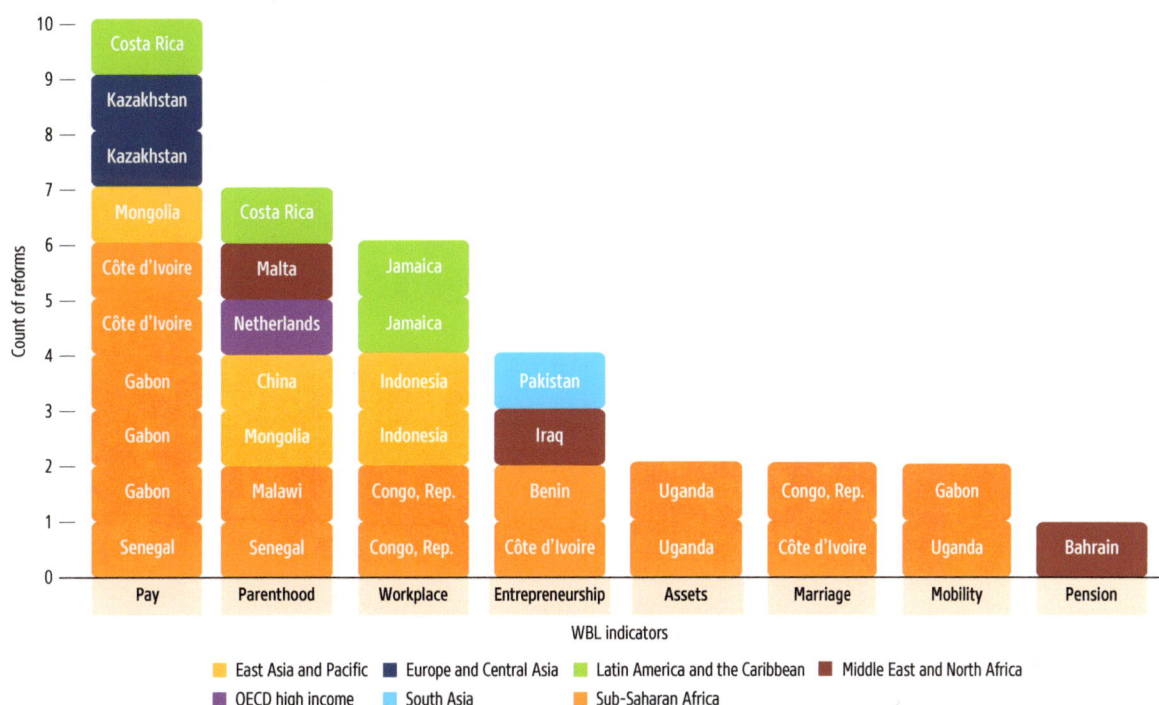

Source: *Women, Business and the Law* database.
Note: OECD = Organisation for Economic Co-operation and Development.

Within the Pay indicator, six economies in four regions enacted reforms that lift restrictions on hiring women or introduce equal remuneration for work of equal value. Costa Rica, Côte d'Ivoire, Gabon, Kazakhstan, and Senegal removed restrictions on women's work. Gabon and Mongolia introduced provisions mandating equal remuneration for work of equal value. Sub-Saharan African economies enacted a breadth of reforms not present in other regions, encompassing seven of the eight indicators.

Two economies enacted laws diminishing equality. In March 2022, Saudi Arabia enacted its first codified personal status law, which regulates matters related to family life. The law restricts a married woman's ability to choose where to live and travel, and it further requires her to obey her husband. Saudi Arabia previously enacted legislation to protect women from sexual harassment and prohibit gender discrimination in employment and access to finance, and it eliminated all restrictions on women's employment. In 2019, Saudi Arabia allowed women to be head of household, removed the legal obligation for a married woman to obey her husband, and improved women's mobility by removing restrictions on obtaining a passport and traveling abroad. Legal amendments also equalized a woman's right to choose where to live and to leave the marital home. However, the personal status law promulgated by Royal Decree M73 reintroduced some of the restrictions into the law.

The interim Taliban administration in Afghanistan issued guidelines and decrees also limiting women's freedom of movement and ability to get a job (annex 1B). The recent regime change in the country has negatively affected both the economy and the welfare of the Afghan people, in particular, women and girls. Access to secondary education for girls has been significantly constrained, and nearly half of women in salaried work have lost their employment (World Bank 2022a). More recently, the government suspended university education for all female students and barred women from working in nongovernmental organizations in the country. Many of these restrictions are imposed by verbal decree and remain unpublished by an official source. Given the uncertainty over the applicable legal framework in Afghanistan, and because unwritten rules are not considered under the *Women, Business and the Law* methodology, the final count of changes widening the legal gender gap there are based only on what is identifiable in writing.

Mobility

Women's agency through freedom of movement, as measured by the Mobility indicator, is a fundamental first step toward economic empowerment. Mobility tracks differences in the laws and regulations that govern the rights of men and women to choose where to live, travel outside the home, obtain a passport, and leave the marital home at will. Constraining a woman's physical mobility, often justified as a way to ensure her safety, affects a woman's bargaining position in the household and can lead to her lower participation in the economic and political spheres (Milazzo and Goldstein 2019). For example, limitations on a woman's mobility are likely to influence her decision to enter the labor force and to engage in entrepreneurial activity (Htun, Jensenius, and Nelson-Nuñez 2019). Conversely, removing restrictions on mobility can provide a woman with better employment opportunities (Hallward-Driemeier and Gajigo 2015). For example, Hallward-Driemeier and Gajigo (2015) show that changes in Ethiopia's family law strengthened a woman's economic rights and made it more likely that she would work outside the home. Furthermore, removing travel restrictions not only encourages a woman's entry into the private sector workforce, but also increases her likelihood of becoming a business owner (Islam, Muzi, and Amin 2019).

Although Mobility has the lowest number of restrictions among all *Women, Business and the Law* indicators, 55 economies worldwide continue to limit a woman's freedom of movement. Two of these—the Islamic Republic of Iran and South Sudan—score 0 on this indicator. In 14 economies, a woman cannot freely leave the home, and in 10 economies a woman cannot travel abroad in the same way as a man (table 1.3). In 34 economies, a woman cannot freely choose where to live in the same way as a man. In April 2022, Uganda enacted a reform in this area by adopting the Succession (Amendment) Act, which, in addition to equalizing inheritance rights, allows a married woman to choose where to live.

Constraints on a woman's mobility may also be due to discriminatory and more burdensome access to formal identification documents. In 28 economies, women are still required to present additional documentation when applying for a passport. In alignment with the country's Equality Strategy, Gabon reformed in this area by making passport application procedures equal for men and women. Previously, Gabon required the husband's authorization when issuing a passport to a married woman.

TABLE 1.3	NUMBER OF ECONOMIES WITH ROOM TO REFORM LAWS GUARANTEEING A WOMAN'S FREEDOM OF MOVEMENT			
Question	Economies with a "yes"		Economies with a "no"	
	Number of economies	Percentage of economies	Number of economies	Percentage of economies
1. Can a woman choose where to live in the same way as a man?	156	82	34	18
2. Can a woman travel outside her home in the same way as a man?	176	93	14	7
3. Can a woman apply for a passport in the same way as a man?	162	85	28	15
4. Can a woman travel outside the country in the same way as a man?	180	95	10	5

Source: Women, Business and the Law database.

Now, a woman is no longer required to provide this authorization or a copy of her husband's identity card when applying for a passport.

In contrast to these amendments enhancing gender parity, Afghanistan and Saudi Arabia enacted laws that reduce gender equality in the area of Mobility. The interim Taliban administration in Afghanistan introduced legal restrictions on a woman's ability to travel abroad without a male chaperone. Saudi Arabia's first personal status law, based on the rules of Islam's Sharia law, regulates issues related to marriage, divorce, and custody of children. The law now includes restrictions on a married woman's ability to choose where to live and to travel.

Workplace

The Workplace indicator analyzes laws affecting a woman's decision to enter the labor market, including her legal capacity and ability to work as well as protections against discrimination and sexual harassment. Evidence shows that a woman's inability to choose her profession freely is negatively associated with her chances of employment (Gonzales et al. 2015) and that the removal of legal barriers can encourage a woman's participation in paid employment and in jobs requiring higher levels of education (Hallward-Driemeier and Gajigo 2015). Moreover, data from the United States show that sexual harassment in the workplace can negatively affect a woman's career trajectory and increase financial stress (McLaughlin, Uggen, and Blackstone 2017).

In 69 economies, a woman faces obstacles affecting her decision to work, such as not being able to choose whether to work and not being protected from discrimination and sexual harassment in employment. In 19 economies, a woman cannot get a job in the same way as a man. In December 2021, the interim Taliban administration in Afghanistan issued a ban on women's ability to work. Now, Afghan women are mostly restricted from working outside the home.

Discrimination in employment is also a barrier to a woman's ability to get a job and to progress in a career. Although antidiscrimination legislation is positively associated with a woman's employment and earnings, in 30 economies gender discrimination in

TABLE 1.4	NUMBER OF ECONOMIES WITH ROOM TO REFORM LAWS PROTECTING WOMEN IN THE WORKPLACE			
Question	Economies with a "yes"		Economies with a "no"	
	Number of economies	Percentage of economies	Number of economies	Percentage of economies
1. Can a woman get a job in the same way as a man?	171	90	19	10
2. Does the law prohibit discrimination in employment based on gender?	160	84	30	16
3. Is there legislation on sexual harassment in employment?	147	77	43	23
4. Are there criminal penalties or civil remedies for sexual harassment in employment?	139	73	51	27

Source: Women, Business and the Law database.

employment is still not prohibited (table 1.4). This number remained unchanged over the past year—that is, no economy implemented reforms in this area.

Sexual harassment in the workplace remains pervasive and continues to have regressive effects on women across the world. In addition to its physical and psychological impacts on women (Thurston et al. 2019), sexual harassment contributes to the gender wage gap (Folke and Rickne 2022; Hegewisch, Forden, and Mefferd 2021). Lower employee productivity, lower company profitability, and higher labor costs are some of the economic and social consequences of sexual harassment borne by employers, governments, and society as a whole (Hejase 2021). For example, a study conducted in Australia found that lost output deriving from sexual harassment cases totals about US$2 billion annually (Deloitte Access Economics 2019).

Yet globally, 43 economies still lack legislation addressing sexual harassment in employment. Of the 147 economies that have such legislation, 8 do not have criminal penalties or civil remedies for such behavior. Over the last year, the Republic of Congo, Indonesia, and Jamaica implemented reforms in this area. In May 2022, the Republic of Congo adopted the Law Mouebara, which addresses and criminalizes multiple forms of violence against women, including sexual harassment in employment. Indonesia's 2022 Law on the Crime of Sexual Violence addresses both physical and nonphysical sexual harassment in employment and provides for criminal penalties and civil remedies. Jamaica adopted legislation exclusively addressing sexual harassment—the Sexual Harassment (Protection and Prevention) Act 2021, which also establishes civil remedies for survivors of such acts.

Pay

The Pay indicator examines whether laws are in place to ensure equal remuneration between men and women for work of equal value and whether they allow a woman to work at night, in industrial jobs, and in jobs deemed dangerous in the same way as a man. Gender biases and inequalities that have placed women in low-wage occupations, such as differences in jobs and hours worked, as well as women's disproportionate caregiving responsibilities, contribute to the gender wage gap. The persistence of this income disparity between men and women negatively affects the growth of a country's economy. Globally, in 119 economies legal frameworks could be improved to contribute to reducing the gender pay gap.

TABLE 1.5	NUMBER OF ECONOMIES WITH ROOM TO REFORM LAWS ADDRESSING THE GENDER PAY GAP				
Question		Economies with a "yes"		Economies with a "no"	
		Number of economies	Percentage of economies	Number of economies	Percentage of economies
1. Does the law mandate equal remuneration for work of equal value?		97	51	93	49
2. Can a woman work at night in the same way as a man?		169	89	21	11
3. Can a woman work in a job deemed dangerous in the same way as a man?		141	74	49	26
4. Can a woman work in an industrial job in the same way as a man?		125	66	65	34

Source: Women, Business and the Law database.

Ninety-seven economies mandate equal remuneration for work of equal value (table 1.5). Over the last year, Gabon and Mongolia adopted new labor laws introducing the principle of equal remuneration for work of equal value for both men and women in alignment with the ILO Equal Remuneration Convention, 1951 (No. 100).

The adoption of more equal laws pertaining to a woman's access to the workforce is positively associated with more equal labor market outcomes and improved human capital, which cannot be met only by male workers (Rostiyanti, Hansen, and Harison 2020). Restricting a woman's occupational choices leads not only to job segregation, but also to labor market distortions, lower wages for women, and less innovation and productivity (Blau and Kahn 2017). Prohibiting a woman from working the night shift may negatively affect her career progression (Islam, Muzi, and Amin 2019). Currently, 21 economies limit a woman's capacity to work at night. In 49 economies, a woman cannot work in hazardous jobs, and in 65 economies she cannot work in the same industries as a man (table 1.6).

Over the last year, Costa Rica, Côte d'Ivoire, Gabon, Kazakhstan, and Senegal eliminated restrictions on women's job opportunities. In March 2022, Costa Rica adopted the Decree for the Freedom of Employment Choice of Women, which reformed the labor code by lifting restrictions on women's work in jobs deemed dangerous. The restriction now affects only persons under the age of 18. Côte d'Ivoire also reformed in this area by adopting Decree No. 2021-919, which not only allows women to work in jobs classified as dangerous, but also removes restrictions on the employment

TABLE 1.6	SIXTY-FIVE ECONOMIES PROHIBIT WOMEN FROM PERFORMING CERTAIN TASKS	
Industry	Economies with at least one restriction	Examples of restrictions
Agriculture	18	Manufacture of fertilizers and insecticides (Angola, Kuwait, Syrian Arab Republic)
Construction	29	Work on a scaffold of 10 meters or more above the ground (Thailand)
Energy	21	Exploratory drilling of oil and gas wells (Russian Federation)
Manufacturing	43	Greasing and cleaning of moving machinery, handling of belts, circular saws (Argentina)
Mining	54	Work underground in mines, quarries, and galleries (Cameroon)
Transportation	15	Work in railway or road transportation and civil aviation (Tajikistan)
Water	20	Work underground or under water, such as mine hearths, cable laying, sewerage, and tunnel construction (Türkiye)

Source: Women, Business and the Law database.

of women in certain types of jobs and industries. Gabon enacted a new labor code, which, by repealing the previous one, lifted all restrictions on a woman's capacity to work in certain industries and hazardous jobs. Kazakhstan amended its labor code and removed the list of jobs restricted to women as well as a prohibition on their work under dangerous conditions. Similarly, Senegal adopted Decree No. 2021-1469, which removed restrictions to employing women who are not pregnant and not nursing in certain industries.

Marriage

The Marriage indicator assesses legal constraints related to marriage and divorce, which also have critical effects on women's economic empowerment. Where and while these constraints persist, women's agency and decision-making powers within the household are weakened (Branisa, Klasen, and Ziegler 2013). Currently, women continue to face such restrictions in 89 economies. Family matters such as marriage and divorce, as well as other domestic issues such as domestic violence, are often considered private and determined by social norms and beliefs regarding a woman's role in society—one that is typically limited to the household. Reforming inherently private matters such as marriage is often met with opposition under the guise of protecting national or cultural identity. This antagonism cements the power equilibrium between men and women, with tangible consequences for women's economic empowerment.

Research shows that restraining a woman's ability to become head of household may negatively affect the representation of women in the labor force (Gonzales et al. 2015). Laws constraining women from becoming head of household diminish women's legal capacity and economic autonomy and may exclude them from public decision-making in multiple domains, such as the water sector (box 1.4). Where only husbands can become head of household, they are unilaterally assigned intrahousehold decision-making and given authority to make decisions on behalf of the family or to administer finances and assets exclusively (Hallward-Driemeier and Hasan 2013). When women have less bargaining power at home, their capacity to pursue professional roles outside their household is constrained (Htun, Jensenius, and Nelson-Nuñez 2019). This adverse power dynamic is aggravated when women cannot end a marriage because they do not have equal divorce rights (Christopherson et al. 2022). Unequal rights in marriage and divorce can further jeopardize women's financial security (Voena 2015). In turn, recent research has shown that domestic violence legislation is associated with reduced mortality for women (Amin, Islam, and Lopez-Claros 2021). By the same token, research has also shown that political stability is a key factor affecting the implementation of these policies, since people need the policies to be in place for long enough to be able to commit to deviating from the norm (Poyker 2021).

In the past year, no economy enacted reforms allowing women to be head of household in the same way as a man, resulting in 28 economies maintaining such a restriction (table 1.7). Similarly, no economy instituted reforms making it easier for women to divorce or remarry. Women remain unable to obtain a divorce in the same way as men in 46 economies. And globally, women in 68 economies face restrictions on their ability to remarry. Specifically, a woman is required to observe a waiting period varying between 90 and 365 days or prove that she is not pregnant before remarriage, whereas no conditions are placed on a man's remarriage. For example, although Benin

BOX 1.4 WOMEN'S RIGHTS AND CONSTRAINTS RELATED TO THE WATER SECTOR

Access to clean water is essential for human well-being, and women play a central role in the provision, management, and safeguarding of water (Ray 2007). Climate change has a significant impact on water resources, and this impact is often felt disproportionally by women and girls (UN 2022). In many economies, women and girls bear the responsibility for collecting water for their households, which can result in lost time and opportunities for work, education, and leisure. As water becomes scarce and weather patterns change, women and girls are often responsible for collecting water from farther away or during more dangerous conditions. Climate change also creates more pressure on water, affecting the productivity of the agriculture sector, which is often the main source of income and food security for many women in developing economies (Mbwo et al. 2019).

Laws measured by *Women, Business and the Law* can have enabling or restricting implications for women's access to water and related infrastructure. For instance, laws preventing women from being head of household or owning land may adversely affect women's access to water and sanitation services; they may also systematically exclude women from participating in decision-making institutions related to water management where such power may be a formal or informal prerequisite (Meinzen-Dick and Zwarteveen 1998; van Koppen 2001). Growing evidence shows that equal participation of women in such decision-making institutions is positively associated with better water management, better-functioning water systems, expanded access, and economic and environmental benefits (Imburgia et al. 2020; Najjar, Baruahb, and El Garhi 2019).[a] In addition to facing tangible barriers of representation in water management, laws can also constrain women from working in typically male-dominated sectors, including several areas related to water. Specifically, laws can create barriers for women regarding type of work and work hours.

As of today, women are restricted from working in areas related to water in 20 economies.[b] Restrictions are in place across five regions, with the largest gaps concentrated in the Eastern Europe and Central Asia region, followed by Sub-Saharan Africa. For example, women in the Kyrgyz Republic cannot work as divers performing underwater work, such as plumbing blasters or pipe grinders, and cannot work repairing or cleaning sewer systems and trenches. Similarly, in Nigeria, women are prevented from working at night in sewers or water works. Globally, women tend to be underrepresented in the water sector, with less than one in five water workers being a woman (World Bank 2019b). The gender gap in water-related employment needs to be addressed in order to reach international commitments on water and sanitation for all (World Bank 2019).

a. While not measured by *Women, Business and the Law*, economies across regions specifically enshrine gender quotas into law, ensuring gender-balanced decision-making bodies—for example, Honduras in Acuerdo 300-2017 on Basin Organizations; Nepal in Irrigation Rules, 2056 (2000); or Namibia in Water Resource Management Act, 2013.
b. Azerbaijan, Bangladesh, Belarus, Belize, China, Dominica, Kyrgyz Republic, Madagascar, Malaysia, Nigeria, Papua New Guinea, the Russian Federation, Sierra Leone, Somalia, St. Kitts and Nevis, St. Vincent and the Grenadines, Sudan, Tajikistan, Thailand, and Türkiye.

TABLE 1.7	NUMBER OF ECONOMIES WITH ROOM TO REFORM LAWS RELATED TO MARRIAGE AND DIVORCE			
Question	Economies with a "yes"		Economies with a "no"	
	Number of economies	Percentage of economies	Number of economies	Percentage of economies
1. Is the law free of legal provisions that require a married woman to obey her husband?	172	91	18	9
2. Can a woman be head of household in the same way as a man?	162	85	28	15
3. Is there legislation specifically addressing domestic violence?	162	85	28	15
4. Can a woman obtain a judgment of divorce in the same way as a man?	144	76	46	24
5. Does a woman have the same rights to remarry as a man?	122	64	68	36

Source: Women, Business and the Law database.

recently removed a 300-day waiting period for women, it continues to require them to prove that they are not pregnant before they can legally remarry.

Positive reforms under the Marriage indicator were enacted in the area of domestic violence, with the Republic of Congo and Côte d'Ivoire introducing legislation addressing this issue for the first time. In the Republic of Congo, women now enjoy legal protections against various forms of domestic violence, including physical, sexual, psychological, and economic abuse. Violators of this law can face criminal penalties, including imprisonment, and protection orders are available for survivors. Côte d'Ivoire, through the enactment of the Law Mouebara, addressed various forms of domestic violence, including physical, sexual, and psychological abuse. At the same time, Côte d'Ivoire amended its penal code, which now imposes strict penalties for acts of domestic violence.

Domestic violence is a deprivation of agency that, besides its negative impact on women's health and ability to participate actively in the labor force, leads to economic costs that are estimated at 5 percent of global gross domestic product (Yount et al. 2022). Recent research shows that the negative effect of violence against women on economic development is aggravated in countries that also lack protective laws against domestic violence. Adopting and reinforcing laws against domestic violence, in addition to strengthening women's decision-making power, could help to curb the prevalence of domestic violence and its related economic costs (Ouedraogo and Stenzel 2021). Further, it would improve women's well-being in the workplace and increase their probability of being promoted and earning higher salaries (Gu, Li, and Peng 2022). Implementing domestic violence legislation is, therefore, critical to improving women's participation in the labor force.

Although the pace of reform in this area is largely positive, one economy enacted legislation limiting women's rights in marriage. Saudi Arabia's Personal Status Law of 2022 requires married women to obey their husbands. The law is not a regional exception; similar practices are codified in personal status laws in neighboring economies. For example, Bahrain, the Arab Republic of Egypt, and Kuwait still legally require married women to obey their husbands.

Parenthood

The Parenthood indicator examines laws affecting a woman's work during and after pregnancy, including paid leave, and laws prohibiting firms from dismissing workers because they are pregnant (table 1.8). Although 7 economies enacted reforms in this area over the past year, the law in 155 economies has gaps affecting a woman's work after having children. The highest-scoring regions in this area are OECD high income (94.7) and Europe and Central Asia (80.9), and the lowest are Middle East and North Africa (35.0) and South Asia (30.0).

Before a woman gives birth, protection from dismissal due to pregnancy is crucial, as established in the ILO Maternity Protection Convention, 2000 (No. 183). Protection of pregnant employees is essential to encouraging women to participate in the workforce. Employment protection during pregnancy ensures that women are not unfairly dismissed or discriminated against because of their biological ability to bear children (Behari 2021). In the past year, Senegal amended its Labor Code and introduced a provision that prohibits the dismissal of pregnant workers. Yet 41 economies still do not prohibit the dismissal of pregnant women.

TABLE 1.8	NUMBER OF ECONOMIES WITH ROOM TO REFORM LAWS INCENTIVIZING A WOMAN TO WORK AFTER HAVING CHILDREN			
Question	Economies with a "yes"		Economies with a "no"	
	Number of economies	Percentage of economies	Number of economies	Percentage of economies
1. Is paid leave of at least 14 weeks available to mothers?	118	62	72	38
2. Does the government administer 100% of maternity leave benefits?	99	52	91	48
3. Is paid leave available to fathers?	117	62	73	38
4. Is there paid parental leave?	53	28	137	72
5. Is dismissal of pregnant workers prohibited?	149	78	41	22

Source: Women, Business and the Law database.

The need for policy intervention also remains critical after a woman bears a child. Indeed, studies show a positive and statistically significant relationship between maternity leave and female employment (Del Boca, Pasqua, and Pronzato 2009; Ruhm 1998). The positive relationship is even stronger when maternity leave is fully funded by the government rather than being underwritten by the employer (Amin and Islam 2022). Seventy-two economies do not mandate at least 14 weeks of paid maternity leave as set out by the 2000 ILO Maternity Protection Convention. The count is the same as last year, as over the past year, none of them introduced new paid maternity leave policies or increased existing ones to reach 14 weeks. Currently, 118 economies grant working mothers paid maternity leave of at least 14 weeks. However, of these economies, only 80 provide maternity benefits through public funds such as social security. In 15 economies, the cost of maternity benefits is covered solely by the employer, while in 23 economies the cost is shared by employers and the government.

Although job-protected maternity leave of adequate length and pay is critical, offering only leave for mothers, especially above a threshold of 30 weeks, can be correlated with fewer women in the workforce (Del Rey, Kyriacou, and Silva 2021). Studies show that a smaller gap between mothers' and fathers' leave is associated with a higher female labor force participation rate, suggesting that women's participation in the workforce could be increased by shrinking the leave gap between parents (Hyland and Shen 2022). Globally, 117 economies provide fathers with paid leave for the birth of a child. Although a similar number of economies provide both maternity leave (118) and paternity leave (117), the length of leave differs drastically, with an average of 192.3 days for mothers and just 22.5 days for fathers.

Over the past year, three economies introduced paid paternity leave for the first time. Costa Rica now grants new fathers leave of two days a week at full salary for the first four weeks after the birth of a child. Fathers in Malawi are now entitled to two weeks of paid paternity leave with full pay. And Mongolia grants at least 10 working days of leave to new fathers, also with full payment of the worker's salary.

As for parental leave—that is, leave available for either parent—53 economies have adopted relevant legislation. Since October 2021, China, Malta, and the Netherlands have introduced paid parental leave policies that help parents to share care duties after childbirth. China introduced a parental leave policy that allocates five days of paid parental leave to each parent each year at full pay until their child reaches age 3. The Work-Life Balance for Parents and Carers Regulation in Malta grants each parent the individual right to take two months of paid leave with half pay and an additional two months of unpaid leave. In the Netherlands, each parent is now entitled to nine weeks of paid parental leave, equivalent to 63 calendar days, at 70 percent of the employee's daily wage. With this reform, the country now scores 100 in the *Women, Business and the Law* index.

Entrepreneurship

Because running a business is an alternative to wage employment and often the preferred choice for women, the Entrepreneurship indicator examines barriers to a woman's ability to start and run a business. Unequal legal treatment of women poses a significant barrier to female entrepreneurs and to women who plan to start a business (see, for example, Htun, Jensenius, and Nelson-Nuñez 2019; Hyland and Islam 2021). Starting a business constitutes an important avenue for women's economic empowerment. While entrepreneurship is an equally important path to prosperity for men, women face significantly more barriers (for an overview, De Vita, Mari, and Poggesi 2014). As a result, women are less likely to become entrepreneurs, with 68 women entrepreneurs for every 100 men entrepreneurs active globally (GEM 2022). Recent estimates suggest that the gender gap is highest in lower-income economies. This disparity may have been exacerbated by the COVID-19 pandemic, as women-led businesses were hit disproportionately hard and were also less likely to receive public support (Torres et al. 2021). Similarly, women-owned firms, while more likely to have applied for a loan during the COVID-19 pandemic, were more than twice as likely to have their application rejected than men-owned firms (Hyland et al. 2021). Policies that promote women's access to finance, especially by reducing the requirements for collateral, are important tools to increase the productivity and resilience of women-owned firms (Hess, Klapper, and Beegle 2021; Ubfal 2022). Removing constraints to women's entrepreneurship can have a significant impact on economic inclusion. Although 89 economies achieve the highest score under the Entrepreneurship indicator, in many economies women still face legal constraints in access to finance, limiting their chances to become successful entrepreneurs (table 1.9). For example, estimates by the International Finance Corporation indicate that female entrepreneurs have an unmet demand for credit of US$1.7 trillion (IFC 2017).

TABLE 1.9	NUMBER OF ECONOMIES WITH ROOM TO REFORM BARRIERS TO WOMEN'S ENTREPRENEURSHIP				
Question		Economies with a "yes"		Economies with a "no"	
		Number of economies	Percentage of economies	Number of economies	Percentage of economies
1. Does the law prohibit discrimination in access to credit based on gender?		89	47	101	53
2. Can a woman sign a contract in the same way as a man?		188	99	2	1
3. Can a woman register a business in the same way as a man?		185	97	5	3
4. Can a woman open a bank account in the same way as a man?		184	97	6	3

Source: Women, Business and the Law database.

To date, 101 economies still lack legal provisions that expressly prohibit gender-based discrimination in access to credit. The absence of this prohibition is evident in all regions, with 88 percent of economies in South Asia showing gaps in this area, 71 percent in Sub-Saharan Africa, 68 percent in East Asia and Pacific, 66 percent in Latin America and the Caribbean, 55 percent in the Middle East and North Africa, 26 percent in Europe and Central Asia, and 15 percent among OECD high-income economies.

Since October 2021, however, Benin, Côte d'Ivoire, and Iraq have taken steps to reduce discrimination in access to financial services. Benin's Ministry of Finance first issued a circular to prohibit gender-based discrimination in access to credit just for microfinance institutions. Then in September 2022, the government issued a ministerial order expanding the scope of the circular to all financial institutions. Similarly, Côte d'Ivoire amended its penal code, now mandating that goods, credit, or services be provided without discrimination based on sex. As for Iraq, its reform efforts to prohibit gender-based discrimination in access to credit are part of the central bank's commitment to enhancing financial inclusion. With the issuance of a central bank circular, Iraq joins regional reform efforts to include women financially through central bank regulations. Over the last three years, *Women, Business and the Law* captured a majority of similar legislative reforms in economies in the Middle East and North Africa, including in Bahrain, Egypt, Jordan, Saudi Arabia, and the United Arab Emirates.

The ability to sign a contract, open a bank account, and freely register a business are also important for a woman's agency and ability to establish her own business. Of the 190 economies measured, a woman can now sign a contract in the same way as a man in all but two—Equatorial Guinea and Eswatini. Six economies—Cameroon, Chad, Equatorial Guinea, Eswatini, Guinea-Bissau, and Niger—restrict a woman's ability to open a bank account in the same way as a man. And five economies—Equatorial Guinea, Eswatini, Guinea-Bissau, Kenya, and Suriname—still restrict a woman's capacity to register a business freely. In Pakistan, a May 2019 presidential ordinance initially repealed discriminatory provisions on registering a business. Yet these repeals did not become operational, as the Senate and National Assembly did not ratify the ordinance before its expiration after 120 days. In December 2021, Pakistan removed these restrictions, and a married woman no longer needs to present her husband's name when registering a business. This amendment concluded Pakistan's previous reform efforts to remove the restriction.

Assets

Given the central role that property can play in women's economic opportunity, the Assets indicator examines gender differences in property and inheritance law. Women's ownership, use, and control over resources matter for their agency and economic output (O'Sullivan 2017). Empirical studies suggest that an egalitarian distribution of assets between spouses is conducive to women's intrahousehold decision-making (Behrman 2017). Strengthening inheritance rights for women, for instance, has positive implications for women's education and health outcomes (Deininger et al. 2019). Further, women's property rights are also important for several other development outcomes, such as empowerment and the ability to exit poverty (Gaddis, Lahoti, and

Swaminathan 2022). The ability to register land in a woman's name, for example, has been found to increase her bargaining power and ownership of assets, which, in turn, positively affects her consumption choices, participation in labor markets, and overall productivity (Deininger and Ali 2022). Access to land and property rights are often also prerequisites for other rights such as accessing water. Still, women face various barriers to owning and inheriting assets worldwide.

Of the 190 economies studied, 76 still restrict a woman's property rights. The highest-scoring regions on the Assets indicator are Europe and Central Asia, OECD high income, and Latin America and the Caribbean. The Middle East and North Africa region lags behind.

Globally, 57 economies do not recognize a woman's nonmonetary contributions to a household (table 1.10). Because women perform most unpaid care and household work, their opportunities to look for a job and gain independent living are often limited. Recognizing unpaid work is thus key for women having economic autonomy on the dissolution of marriage.

Nineteen economies do not grant women equal ownership rights to immovable property, and 18 do not grant women the right to control jointly owned assets. Yet studies have shown that granting a woman equal rights to property is crucial to improving her economic empowerment.

Equal inheritance rights among spouses or children are also central to women's economic independence and ability to access credit by using immovable property as collateral. Currently, 41 economies still differentiate inheritance rights between sons and daughters, favoring sons in the division of property. And 43 economies still do not grant equal inheritance rights to male and female surviving spouses.

In 2022, only Uganda instituted new reforms under the Assets indicator. In April, Uganda enacted the Succession (Amendment) Act, thereby amending the principal act,[2] which regulates the management, administration, distribution, and acquisition of property and the rights of a deceased person. In 2007, the Constitutional Court declared several provisions of the Principal Act related to succession rights to be unconstitutional and discriminatory against women.[3] The new Succession (Amendment) Act aims to fill this legal void in the succession law. In addition to adopting gender-neutral language, the amendment specifically removes the provision that favored a male heir over a

TABLE 1.10	NUMBER OF ECONOMIES WITH ROOM TO REFORM LAWS GRANTING WOMEN EQUAL RIGHTS TO PROPERTY AND INHERITANCE			
Question	Economies with a "yes"		Economies with a "no"	
	Number of economies	Percentage of economies	Number of economies	Percentage of economies
1. Do men and women have equal ownership rights to immovable property?	171	90	19	10
2. Do sons and daughters have equal rights to inherit assets from their parents?	149	78	41	22
3. Do male and female surviving spouses have equal rights to inherit assets?	147	77	43	23
4. Does the law grant spouses equal administrative authority over assets during marriage?	172	91	18	9
5. Does the law provide for the valuation of nonmonetary contributions?	133	70	57	30

Source: Women, Business and the Law database.

female heir. Now, sons and daughters and male and female surviving spouses have equal inheritance rights.

Historically, inheritance has been an area of slow reform. With the new Succession (Amendment) Act, Uganda became the first Sub-Saharan African economy to implement comprehensive reforms of its inheritance laws since 2011, when Mali equalized inheritance rights for men and women.

Pension

Recognizing the final step in a woman's career, the Pension indicator assesses laws affecting women's economic security after retirement. In 118 economies, laws affecting the size of a woman's pension have not yet been equalized. Eleven economies do not implement a mandatory pension scheme for private sector workers; thus, no score is assigned to these economies in the questions under the Pension indicator.[4]

Differences in the working lives of men and women stemming from career interruptions for care- or household-related responsibilities significantly affect the size of their old-age pensions. Evidence reveals that in Germany, if the pattern of interrupted careers remains unchanged, women's pensions will be 20 percent less than the average wage, while in Sweden women's pensions barely exceed 25 percent of the average wage. Thus, if old-age income relied solely on pensions linked to life course earnings, women would face a high risk of poverty after retirement (Chłon-Dominczak et al. 2019).

Because women tend to live longer than men and have shorter working lives due to unpaid care work, early retirement can have negative effects on a woman's financial security in old age. Women may experience peak earnings years before retirement and, as a result, forgo opportunities to build savings and increase social security benefit entitlements (Goldin and Katz 2018). Evidence also reveals a clear association between the length of working life and pension income. The longer the working life, the higher the monthly pension benefit (Kuivalainen, Järnefelt, and Kuitto 2020). Yet in 37 economies, women can retire earlier than men and receive partial pension benefits, and in 63 economies women can retire earlier than men and receive full pension benefits (table 1.11). In 15 economies across all regions except South Asia, women must retire earlier than men.

The gap between a woman's and a man's retirement age varies from 10 years (China) to 7 months (Lithuania). Some economies have introduced policies to increase

TABLE 1.11	NUMBER OF ECONOMIES WITH ROOM TO REFORM LAWS ENSURING A WOMAN'S ECONOMIC SECURITY IN OLD AGE				
Question		Economies with a "yes"		Economies with a "no"	
		Number of economies	Percentage of economies	Number of economies	Percentage of economies
1. Is the age at which men and women can retire with full pension benefits the same?		127	67	63	33
2. Is the age at which men and women can retire with partial pension benefits the same?		153	81	37	19
3. Is the mandatory retirement age for men and women the same?		175	92	15	8
4. Are periods of absence due to childcare accounted for in pension benefits?		107	56	83	44

Source: Women, Business and the Law database.

a woman's retirement age gradually with the goal of equalizing it with a man's. For example, Bulgaria will gradually increase the retirement age for both men and women to 65 years by 2037. For men, the retirement age has been growing one month each calendar year since January 1, 2018. For women, the age will increase two months each calendar year until 2029 and will then increase three months each calendar year until it reaches 65. In Vietnam, however, the retirement ages for men and women will never equalize during the gradual increase. Specifically, Article 169 of the labor code establishes that, as of 2021, the retirement age for men will increase three months per year, reaching 62 years by 2028. By contrast, the retirement age for women will increase four months per year, reaching 60 years by 2035. In the past year, Bahrain amended its Social Insurance Law to equalize the age at which both men and women can receive full pension benefits at retirement. Previously, women in Bahrain retired at 55, five years earlier than men. Now both men and women retire at 60.

In 107 economies, the pension system in place accounts for periods taken off from work to care for children (that is, paid maternity leave) in the calculation of benefits. This calculation is important because the size of a woman's pension is affected by the number and length of interruptions in employment arising from caregiving responsibilities (Boeri and Brugiavini 2009; Jędrzychowska, Kwiecień, and Poprawska 2020). The scope of social policies and maternity leave benefits is critical to determine the position of mothers in the labor market and consequently the pension gap (Brugiavini, Pasini, and Trevisan 2011). Australia and the United States are the only two OECD high-income economies that do not take these periods into account.

What's next?

Fulfilling its commitment to advance legal gender equality and women's economic empowerment, *Women, Business and the Law* continues to pursue a substantial research agenda. Multiple areas of research aimed at expanding the reach of the indicators and considering the myriad challenges affecting women's economic opportunities are being explored.

FIGURE 1.8 | EXPANDING THE SCOPE OF THE *WOMEN, BUSINESS AND THE LAW* INDEX

WBL 2023
Research on childcare, implementation, safety, and other areas

WBL 2024
Publication of new data on childcare, disability, implementation, and safety

WBL 2025
Incorporation of new indicators into WBL index and report

Source: Women, Business and the Law team.

Building on evidence and preliminary data collected and analyzed over the last several years, *Women, Business and the Law 2024* will publish data on new indicators measuring childcare legislation and implementation of the law (figure 1.8). Furthermore, *Women, Business and the Law* is continuing to explore new areas of research based on a review of literature, feedback received, and emerging trends. As a result, the team is expanding data and analysis on measures related to women's safety and embarking on a review of areas in which legal equality has almost been reached, such as, for example, the right of women to sign a contract in the same way as men, now granted by 99 percent of economies. This pilot data set will be published in *Women, Business and the Law 2024* and be integrated fully into the index and report in the 2025 edition. The following sections offer more information about each of the areas in development.

Childcare

The enactment of policies to make childcare available, affordable, and of decent quality is a priority because of their potential to achieve better outcomes for women, children, and the economy overall. In support of this goal, *Women, Business and the Law 2022* presented a pilot data set measuring legal frameworks for the provision of childcare for children ages 0–2 in 95 economies. In the absence of international legal standards, the pilot exercise did not endorse a specific approach to the provision of childcare. Instead, it aimed to fill knowledge gaps and contribute to the policy dialogue by presenting options that governments could support to meet the needs of working mothers and families.

The pilot first examined the existence of overarching childcare legal frameworks and found that they vary widely across regions. For example, nearly all economies in the OECD high-income region and Europe and Central Asia regulate public provision of childcare, while many economies in the Middle East and North Africa and South Asia regulate only childcare services provided by the private sector or by employers. The pilot then looked at whether the law can contribute to making childcare affordable by mandating free provision or financial and nonfinancial support to parents or providers. Findings show that, of the 55 economies in which the law regulates public childcare, about 80 percent do not mandate free provision. Many economies, however, provide parents with financial support that may be conditioned on household income or parental employment status. As for childcare quality, mandated parameters such as teacher-to-child ratios, maximum group size, and licensing vary across economies, with no clear pattern among regions. Since the release of the pilot data, *Women, Business and the Law* has published five regional briefs that offer a closer look at the legal frameworks for childcare provision at the regional level (World Bank 2022c, 2022d, 2022e, 2022f, 2022g).

Women, Business and the Law is currently scaling up the childcare module to 150 economies and validating data through questionnaires administered to experts in the field. The questionnaires supplement the traditional "structure" indicators, which measure the existence of laws and regulations, with new "process" indicators, which capture the instruments designed to support implementation of the law such as universal legal entitlements, action plans, application procedures for financial benefits, lists of providers, inspections, and sanctions for noncompliance with quality standards. The data will be analyzed and presented in *Women, Business and the Law 2024,* and a new Childcare indicator will be added to the *Women, Business and the Law* index in 2025.

New empirical research will also explore associations between childcare laws and their specific attributes and labor market outcomes for women, both globally and by region.

Targeting access to available, affordable, and quality childcare services can have far-reaching positive impacts, not only for women as active participants in the labor market, but also for child development and economic growth. *Women, Business and the Law* data and analysis on childcare aim to shed light on these links and to inform evidence-based policy making in support of these goals.

Measuring the law in practice

Women, Business and the Law remains committed to presenting a fuller picture of the legal environment for women around the world. Although laws are the first step toward guaranteeing gender equality, improper implementation and weak enforcement remain critical barriers to the realization of women's rights and opportunities. In recognition of this gap, *Women, Business and the Law 2022* introduced a new conceptual framework for measuring how the law functions in practice. This "structure-process-outcome" approach examines both supportive frameworks that create an enabling environment for working women and expert opinions of barriers to achieving gender equality on the ground (box 1.5). *Women, Business and the Law* has continued to build on the

---

BOX 1.5 UPDATE ON MEASURING THE LAW IN PRACTICE

After the publication of *Women, Business and the Law 2022,* expert feedback led to substantial refinement of the initial method to measure laws in practice. The "structure-process-outcome" method remains at the heart of the approach, guiding both the definition of process indicators to capture essential policy instruments and the development of expert opinion questions. The process questions have been revised to more directly link the legal index with the process questions designed to measure the implementing mechanisms that governments can take to institutionalize, operationalize, and enforce women's equal rights and opportunities (table B1.5.1). The process questions aim to provide insight into the enabling environment for women entrepreneurs and employees, and may inquire whether

- There are additional judicial or administrative hurdles to women exercising their equal rights;
- The government has taken proactive measures, such as establishing a dedicated entity, allocating budget, or using regulations to put policies in practice;
- Women have access to justice, specialized institutions, or fast-track procedures to enforce their rights; or
- Incentives and procedures make it easy for both women and men to enjoy certain benefits.

TABLE B1.5.1	EXAMPLES OF PROCESS QUESTIONS FOR THE PAY INDICATOR	
Legal index question	**Process question**	**New question**
1. Does the law mandate equal remuneration for work of equal value?	1. Have wage transparency measures been introduced to address the pay gap?	✗
2. Can a woman work at night in the same way as a man?	2. Are there policies in place to protect and improve conditions for all night workers?	✓
3. Can a woman work in a job deemed dangerous in the same way as a man?	3. Is there an entity responsible for defining and supporting the adoption of occupational health and safety policies for dangerous jobs?	✓
4. Can a woman work in an industrial job in the same way as a man?	4. Are employers required to take gender differences into consideration and identify adequate protection measures during the workplace risk assessment process?	✓

Source: Women, Business and the Law team.

(Box continues next page)

BOX 1.5 UPDATE ON MEASURING THE IMPLEMENTATION OF LAWS *(continued)*

Primary data are being collected from a sample of *Women, Business and the Law* local experts in 55 economies, with the intention of scaling to 190 in the next year. As such, the questions identified are broadly applicable and allow for comparability. They are meant to highlight some of the steps necessary to ensure that economic inclusion can be achieved after primary legislation is passed. Nonlegal and informal structures, social norms and attitudes, and behavior of stakeholders will not be measured due to resource and feasibility constraints. Firm-level and household surveys will also not be used at this stage. Outcome indicators will be reviewed separately and are not a focus of this exercise. The preliminary data collected so far are already highlighting good practices across several types of process questions (table B1.5.2).

TABLE B1.5.2	EXAMPLES OF POLICIES THAT FACILITATE EFFECTIVE IMPLEMENTATION OF LAWS
Implementing mechanism	**Examples**
Entity responsible for defining and supporting the adoption of antiharassment policies and measures by employers	Ministries of labor or specialized commissions, such as antidiscrimination commissions, equal opportunities commissions, gender commissions, or human rights commissions
Policies supporting all night workers	Increased compensation, mandatory breaks or rest periods, regular health assessments, limitations on the consecutive number of hours for night shifts, and dedicated transportation (if no public transportation is available)
Time line within which the application for maternity leave must be approved or rejected by the competent authority	Administrative time lines mandated by law, which currently range broadly, between a minimum of 15 days and a maximum of 60 days for the competent authority to approve or reject maternity leave applications
Enforcement guidance on the prohibition of dismissal of pregnant workers	As common in legal frameworks in Latin America, the prior authorization by a competent judge for the employer to be able to proceed with the dismissal of a pregnant worker, on exceptional and well-founded grounds, clearly detailed in the legislation
Incentives or programs to encourage women's land tenure security	Mandatory joint titling for married couples and lower property taxes for joint owners or female owners

Source: Women, Business and the Law team.

The expert opinion component has also been adjusted in response to feedback received last year (table B1.5.3). The questions are now aligned more closely with the specific expertise of the lawyers, judges, and civil society organizations who participate in the project's annual data collection efforts. In practice, the expert opinion statements now collect respondents' opinions on the effective implementation of laws and supportive frameworks in the specific areas measured by *Women, Business and the Law*.

TABLE B1.5.3	NEW FORMAT OF THE EXPERT OPINION COMPONENT
Sample statement	**Response options**
In your experience, laws, supportive frameworks, and practice effectively ensure that women have recourse in instances of domestic violence.	• Strongly agree • Agree • Neither agree nor disagree • Disagree • Strongly disagree • Not within my expertise

Source: Women, Business and the Law team.

The current set of questions, methodology, and approach will continue to be refined before the research is expanded to all of the 190 economies covered by the *Women, Business and the Law* index. The data and analysis of the pilot will be published on the project's website.

underlying concept, aiming to complete the framework by reviewing the relevant literature, developing a robust expert opinion questionnaire, updating questions, and scaling up the database.

Revised questions will be integrated into the next round of *Women, Business and the Law* data collection efforts. The data will then be analyzed as a complement to the legal index, with results for 190 economies discussed as part of *Women, Business and the Law 2024*. An accompanying research paper will further describe the results of the complete data set, including gaps between laws on the books and practice, and correlate process and outcome scores with legal scores and relevant economic outcomes. Continuing this work over the coming years will also include expanding beyond expert opinions to in-depth country analysis and perception-based surveys of women on the ground.

These data and analyses are aimed at promoting informed policy making and encouraging governments to implement laws more efficiently and comprehensively. They will also present an opportunity to measure the impact of reforms on the women they affect in practice. When complete, they will provide users with a more accurate representation of the environment in which women move through their lives and careers. The fully developed framework will then allow legal reforms to have more tangible impacts, boosting women's economic inclusion and labor force participation worldwide.

Women's safety

Violence against women is an extreme denial of agency and has significant costs. It undermines a woman's bodily autonomy and enjoyment of fundamental rights, key elements of a woman's security and freedom. Globally, one in three women—close to 736 million—is subject to physical or sexual violence at some point in her lifetime (WHO 2018). It is estimated that more than 640 million women over the age of 15 have already experienced intimate partner violence (WHO 2018). In addition to direct physical and psychological harm, violence against women is a drain on human capital development, poverty reduction, and growth and poses obstacles to women's economic empowerment. Its individual and macroeconomic repercussions include lower productivity (Ouedraogo and Stenzel 2021) and higher health care and justice costs (Commonwealth Secretariat 2020; EIGE 2021).

In recognition of the alarming rates of violence against women worldwide and its disproportionate impact on women and society, since 2014 *Women, Business and the Law* has been collecting data on legal frameworks addressing this issue. Specifically, it has systematically collected data on two aspects of violence against women: domestic violence and sexual harassment in employment, including any related criminal penalties or civil remedies. However, to improve understanding of the current status of violence against women legislation, *Women, Business and the Law* is piloting the collection and analysis of additional measures of legal protection from gender-based violence against women, including laws and regulations on domestic violence; child marriage (legal age of marriage, exceptions to the minimum age, and remedies); marital rape; sexual harassment in employment, education, and public places; cyber harassment; and female genital mutilation.

To complement this new research and understand how such laws are applied in practice, *Women, Business and the Law* will examine process frameworks to support the implementation of these laws, including the provision of services to women survivors of violence, access to justice, national plans, budgetary commitments, and monitoring and evaluation mechanisms. Both process and outcome questions will undergo consultations with experts on matters of violence against women, and data will subsequently be collected through questionnaires administered to local experts on gender equality and violence against women. *Women, Business and the Law 2024* will present the findings of this pilot exercise, which will inform the design of a new and more comprehensive Safety indicator to be added to the index in 2025. The goal of this research is to provide holistic data and analysis that can better inform the design of effective laws and policies addressing gender-based violence against women.

The rights of women with disabilities

One in five women worldwide has a disability and faces not only the same gender gaps but also barriers to her socioeconomic participation, compared with nondisabled women (World Bank and WHO 2011). As a result, women with disabilities are three times more likely to have unmet health care needs and to be illiterate and two times less likely to be employed and to use the internet than men without disabilities (UNDESA 2018). Women with disabilities also experience gender-based violence and harassment at a greater rate than nondisabled women (World Bank 2019a). For example, a recent study found that women with disabilities across the Global South are nearly twice as likely to have encountered intimate partner violence in the past year than women without disabilities (Chirwa et al. 2020).

As part of the World Bank Group's 10 Commitments on Disability-Inclusive Development, *Women, Business and the Law* has produced data and analysis on legal protections for women with disabilities in 190 economies to understand how laws can protect them from intersectional and multiple discrimination. The first policy brief finds that only one-quarter of economies worldwide explicitly recognize the rights of women with disabilities in their legislation (Braunmiller and Dry 2022a). This finding confirms that laws and policies have neglected the specific needs of women with disabilities by focusing predominantly on gender or disability issues (CRPD Committee 2016). A second brief explores the specific rights of women with disabilities as related to family life, work, and protection from gender-based violence, highlighting some promising practices that can inform policy making and legal reforms across the globe (Braunmiller and Dry 2022b).

Gender dimensions of the business climate

Women, Business and the Law will collaborate closely with the World Bank's Business Enabling Environment (BEE) and Enterprise Survey (ES) projects to identify relevant gender dimensions of the business climate that are not captured by the *Women, Business and the Law* indicators. Examples of such dimensions include regulations on collecting anonymized gender-disaggregated data, firms' practices on gender-based discrimination, women's participation in the judiciary, gender barriers in access to finance, and gender equality facilitation programs. These gender areas fall under regulatory frameworks, public services, and efficiency of the business environment and fit well into the de jure and de facto gender measures of *Women, Business and the Law* (World Bank 2022b). The BEE and ES gender data are envisioned to complement the information collected by *Women, Business and the Law*.

The way forward

Other potential areas will also be explored as part of the team's research agenda. For example, research suggests that tax policies can alleviate gender inequalities but also exacerbate inequalities (Grown and Valodia 2010; Lahey 2018; Stotsky 1997, among others). While this area is receiving renewed attention (Coelho et al. 2022; OECD 2022), a global stocktaking and analysis of the interaction between tax policies and gender equality are missing. In collaboration with other units in the World Bank Group, the *Women, Business and the Law* team plans to address this knowledge gap by piloting an assessment of the gender dimensions of tax policies across the globe.

Moving forward, *Women, Business and the Law* will consider expanding or changing the scope of indicators where data variance across countries is limited. For example, in only two countries a woman cannot sign a contract in the same way as a man, and in only five economies a woman faces limitations on her capacity to register a business. Thus, where good-practice legislation has been adopted across almost all economies, *Women, Business and the Law* will assess whether other barriers remain in that topic area in order to reflect the current state of legal gender equality more accurately.

Notes

1. This research includes Amin and Islam (2015); Htun, Jensenius, and Nelson-Nuñez (2019); Islam, Muzi, and Amin (2019); and Zabalza and Tzannatos (1985). Roy (2019) provides an overview of the evidence linking legal gender equality and women's economic outcomes.
2. See the Succession Act Cap 162, which commenced in 1906.
3. For a thorough overview of the *Law Advocacy for Women in Uganda v. Attorney General*, Constitutional Petitions No. 13/2005 and 05/2006, see https://ulii.org/ug/judgment/supreme-court-uganda/2007/71.
4. The 11 economies that do not have a mandatory pension scheme for private sector workers are Afghanistan, Bangladesh, Bhutan, Eritrea, Lebanon, Myanmar, Qatar, Somalia, South Africa, South Sudan, and West Bank and Gaza.

References

Akrofi, Mark M., Mudasiru Mahama, and Chinedu M. Nevo. 2021. "Nexus between the Gendered Socio-economic Impacts of COVID-19 and Climate Change: Implications for Pandemic Recovery." *SN Social Sciences* 1 (8): 198. doi:10.1007/s43545-021-00207-5.

Amin, Mohammad, and Asif M. Islam. 2015. "Does Mandating Nondiscrimination in Hiring Practices Influence Female Employment? Evidence Using Firm-Level Data." *Feminist Economics* 21 (4): 28–60.

Amin, Mohammad, and Asif M. Islam. 2022. "The Impact of Paid Maternity Leave on Women's Employment." Policy Research Working Paper 10188, World Bank, Washington, DC.

Amin, Mohammad, Asif M. Islam, and Augusto Lopez-Claros. 2021. "Absent Laws and Missing Women: Can Domestic Violence Legislation Reduce Female Mortality?" *Review of Development Economics* 25 (4): 2113–32.

Arekapudi, Nisha Nicole, and Nátalia Mazoni. 2022. "Challenging Entrenched Marital Power in South Africa." Global Indicators Brief 6, World Bank, Washington, DC.

Behari, A. 2021. "Proving a Causal Link between Pregnancy and Dismissal: An Analysis of the Disclosure of Pregnancy and the Protection of Pregnant Employees in the South African Workplace." *Journal of South African Law/Tydskrif vir die Suid-Afrikaanse Reg* 2021 (1): 106–22.

Behrman, Julia Andrea. 2017. "Women's Land Ownership and Participation in Decision-Making about Reproductive Health in Malawi." *Population and Environment* 38 (4): 327–44.

Blau, Francine D., and Lawrence M. Kahn. 2017. "The Gender Wage Gap: Extent, Trends, and Explanations." *Journal of Economic Literature* 55 (3): 789–865.

Boeri, Tito, and Agar Brugiavini. 2009. "Pension Reforms and Women Retirement Plans." *Journal of Population Ageing* 1 (35): 7–30. doi.org/10.1007/s12062-009-9001-9.

Branisa, Boris, Stephan Klasen, and Maria Ziegler. 2013. "Gender Inequality in Social Institutions and Gendered Development Outcomes." *World Development* 45 (May): 252–68.

Braunmiller, Julia Constanze, and Marie Dry. 2022a. "The Importance of Designing Gender and Disability Inclusive Laws: A Survey of Legislation in 190 Economies." Global Indicators Brief 11, World Bank, Washington, DC.

Braunmiller, Julia Constanze, and Marie Dry. 2022b. "Safeguarding the Rights of Women with Disabilities to Family Life, Work, and Protection from Gender-based Violence." Global Indicators Brief 14, World Bank, Washington, DC.

Brugiavini, Agar, Giacomo Pasini, and Elisabetta Trevisan. 2011. "Maternity and Labour Market Outcome: Short and Long Term Effects." In *The Individual and the Welfare State: Life Histories in Europe*, edited by Axel Börsch-Supan, Martina Brandt, Karsten Hank, and Mathis Schröeder, 151–59. Berlin and Heidelberg: Springer. doi.org/10.1007/978-3-642-17472-8_13.

Chirwa, Esnat, Rachel Jewkes, Ingrid Van Der Heijden, and Kristin Dunkle. 2020. "Intimate Partner Violence among Women with and without Disabilities: A Pooled Analysis of Baseline Data from Seven Violence-Prevention Programmes." *BMJ Global Health* 5 (11): e002156.

Chłon-Dominczak, Agnieszka, Marek Góra, Irena E. Kotowska, Iga Magda, Anna Ruzik-Sierdzinska, and Paweł Strzelecki. 2019. "The Impact of Lifetime Events on Pensions: NDC Schemes in Poland, Italy, and Sweden and the Point Scheme in Germany." Social Protection and Jobs Discussion Paper 1918, World Bank, Washington, DC.

Christopherson, Katharine, Audrey Yiadom, Juliet Johnson, Francisca Fernando, Hanan Yazid, and Clara Thiemann. 2022. "Tackling Legal Impediments to Women's Economic Empowerment." IMF Working Paper WP/22/37, International Monetary Fund, Washington, DC.

Coelho, Maria Delgado, Aieshwarya Davis, Alexander D. Klemm, and Carolina Osorio Buitron. 2022. "Gendered Taxes: The Interaction of Tax Policy with Gender Equality." International Monetary Fund, Washington, DC.

Commonwealth Secretariat. 2020. *The Economic Cost of Violence against Women and Girls: A Study of Lesotho*. London: Commonwealth Secretariat.

CRPD Committee (Committee on the Rights of Persons with Disabilities). 2016. "General Comment No. 3 (2016): Article 6: Women and Girls with Disabilities." United Nations, New York.

Deininger, Klaus, and Daniel Ayalew Ali. 2022. "How Urban Land Titling and Registry Reform Affect Land and Credit Markets: Evidence from Lesotho." Policy Research Working Paper 10043, World Bank, Washington, DC.

Deininger, Klaus, Songqing Jin, Hari K. Nagarajan, and Fang Xia. 2019. "Inheritance Law Reform, Empowerment, and Human Capital Accumulation: Second-Generation Effects from India." *Journal of Development Studies* 55 (12): 2549–71.

Del Boca, Daniela, Silvia Pasqua, and Chiara Pronzato. 2009. "Motherhood and Market Work Decisions in Institutional Context: A European Perspective." *Oxford Economic Papers* 61 (Suppl. 1): i147–i171.

Deloitte Access Economics. 2019. *The Economic Costs of Sexual Harassment in the Workplace*. Canberra, Australia: Deloitte Access Economics.

Del Rey, Elena, Andreas Kyriacou, and José I. Silva. 2021. "Maternity Leave and Female Labor Force Participation: Evidence from 159 Countries." *Journal of Population Economics* 34 (3): 803–24. doi.org/10.1007/s00148-020-00806-1.

De Paz, Nieven Carmen, Isis Gaddis, and Miriam Muller. 2021. "Gender and COVID-19: What Have We Learnt, One Year Later." Policy Research Working Paper 9709, World Bank, Washington, DC.

De Vita, Luisa, Michael Mari, and Sara Poggesi. 2014. "Women Entrepreneurs in and from Developing Countries: Evidences from the Literature." *European Management Journal* 32 (3): 451–60.

EIGE (European Institute for Gender Equality). 2021. "The Costs of Gender-Based Violence in the European Union." EIGE. Vilnius. Lithuania.

Folke, Olle, and Johanna Rickne. 2022. "Sexual Harassment and Gender Inequality in the Labor Market." *Quarterly Journal of Economics* 137 (4): 2163–212. doi.org/10.1093/qje/qjac018.

Gaddis, Isabel, Rahul Lahoti, and Hema Swaminathan. 2022. "Women's Legal Rights and Gender Gaps in Property Ownership in Developing Countries." *Population and Development Review* 48 (2): 331–77. doi.org/10.1111/padr.12493.

GEM (Global Entrepreneurship Monitor). 2022. *Global Entrepreneurship Monitor 2021/22 Women's Entrepreneurship Report: From Crisis to Opportunity*. London: GEM.

Goldin, Claudia, and Lawrence F. Katz. 2018. *Women Working Longer: Increased Employment at Older Ages.* Chicago: University of Chicago Press.

Gonzales, Christian, Sonali Jain-Chandra, Kalpana Kochhar, and Monique Newiak. 2015. "Fair Play: More Equal Laws Boost Female Labor Force Participation." IMF Staff Discussion Note SDN/15/02, International Monetary Fund, Washington, DC.

Grown, Caren, and Imraan Valodia, eds. 2010. *Taxation and Gender Equity: A Comparative Analysis of Direct and Indirect Taxes in Developing and Developed Countries.* Ottawa: International Development Research Centre; New York: Routledge.

Gu, Xin, Hao Li, and Langchuan Peng. 2022. "The Anti–Domestic Violence Law and Women's Welfare: Evidence from a Natural Experiment in China." *Journal of Economic Behavior & Organization* 202 (October): 1–16. doi.org/10.1016/j.jebo.2022.07.028.

Halim, Daniel, Michael B. O'Sullivan, and Abhilasha Sahay. 2022. "Thematic Policy Brief on Increasing Female Labor Force Participation." World Bank, Washington, DC.

Hallward-Driemeier, Mary, and Ousman Gajigo. 2015. "Strengthening Economic Rights and Women's Occupational Choice: The Impact of Reforming Ethiopia's Family Law." *World Development* 70 (C): 260–73.

Hallward-Driemeier, Mary, and Tazeen Hasan. 2013. *Empowering Women: Legal Rights and Economic Opportunity in Africa.* Washington, DC: World Bank.

Hegewisch, Ariane, Jessica Forden, and Eve Mefferd. 2021. *Paying Today and Tomorrow: Charting the Financial Costs of Workplace Sexual Harassment.* Washington, DC: Institute for Women's Policy Research. https://iwpr.org/iwpr-publications/paying-today-and-tomorrow-report/.

Hejase, Hussin J. 2021. "The Economics of Sexual Harassment." *Journal of Economics and Economic Education Research* 22 (1): 1–3.

Hess, Jake, Leora Klapper, and Kathleen Beegle. 2021. "Financial Inclusion, Women, and Building Back Better." World Bank, Washington, DC.

Htun, Mala, Francesca R. Jensenius, and Jami Nelson-Nuñez. 2019. "Gender-Discriminatory Laws and Women's Economic Agency." *Social Politics: International Studies in Gender, State, and Society* 26 (2): 193–222. doi:10.1093/sp/jxy042.

Hyland, Marie, and Asif Islam. 2021. "Gendered Laws, Informal Origins, and Subsequent Performance." Policy Research Working Paper 9766, World Bank, Washington, DC.

Hyland, Marie, Nona Karalashvili, Silvia Muzi, and Domenico Viganola. 2021. "Female-Owned Firms during the Covid-19 Crisis." Global Indicators Brief 2, World Bank, Washington, DC.

Hyland, Marie, and Liang Shen. 2022. "The Evolution of Maternity and Paternity Leave Policies over Five Decades: A Global Analysis." Policy Research Working Paper 10215, World Bank, Washington, DC.

IFC (International Finance Corporation). 2017. "MSME Finance Gap: Assessment of the Shortfalls and Opportunities in Financing Micro, Small, and Medium Enterprises in Emerging Markets." IFC, Washington, DC.

ILO (International Labour Organization). 2022. *World Employment and Social Outlook: Trends 2022.* Geneva: ILO.

Imburgia, Laura, Henny Osbahr, Sarah Cardey, and Janet Momsen. 2020. "Inclusive Participation, Self-Governance, and Sustainability: Current Challenges and Opportunities for Women in Leadership of Communal Irrigation Systems." *Environment and Planning E: Nature and Space* 4 (3): 886–914.

Islam, Asif, Silvia Muzi, and Mohammad Amin. 2019. "Unequal Laws and the Disempowerment of Women in the Labour Market: Evidence from Firm-Level Data." *Journal of Development Studies* 55 (5): 822–44. doi:10.1080/00220388.2018.1487055.

Jędrzychowska, Anna, Ilona Kwiecień, and Ewa Poprawska. 2020. "The Motherhood Pension Gap in a Defined Contribution Pension Scheme—The Case of Poland." *Sustainability* 12 (11): 4425. doi.org/10.3390/su12114425.

Kuivalainen, Susan, Satu Järnefelt, and Kati Kuitto. 2020. "Length of Working Life and Pension Income: Empirical Evidence on Gender and Socioeconomic Differences from Finland." *Journal of Pension Economics and Finance* 19 (1): 126–46. doi:10.1017/S1474747218000215.

Lahey, Kathleen. 2018. "Gender, Taxation, and Equality in Developing Countries: Issues and Policy Recommendations." UN Women Discussion Paper, UN Women, New York.

Mbow, Cheikh, Cynthia Rosenzweig, Luis G. Barioni, Tim G. Benton, Mario Herrero, Murukesan Krishnapillai, Emma Liwenga, Prajal Pradhan, Marta G. Rivera-Ferre, Tek Sapkota, Francesco N. Tubiello, and Yinlong Xu. 2019. "Food Security." In *Climate Change and Land: An IPCC Special Report on Climate Change, Desertification, Land Degradation, Sustainable Land Management, Food Security, and Greenhouse Gas Fluxes in Terrestrial Ecosystems,* 437–550. Cambridge, UK: Cambridge University Press. doi.org/10.1017/9781009157988.007.

McLaughlin, Heather, Christopher Uggen, and Amy Blackstone. 2017. "The Economic and Career Effects of Sexual Harassment on Working Women." *Gender and Society* 31 (3): 333–58. doi.org/10.1177/0891243217704631.

Meinzen-Dick, Ruth, and Margreet Zwarteveen. 1998. "Gendered Participation in Water Management: Issues and Illustrations from Water Users' Associations in South Asia." *Agriculture and Human Value* 15 (4): 337–45.

Milazzo, Annamaria, and Markus Goldstein. 2019. "Governance and Women's Economic and Political Participation: Power Inequalities, Formal Constraints, and Norms." *World Bank Research Observer* 34 (1): 34–64. doi.org/10.1093/wbro/lky006.

Najjar, Dina, Bipasha Baruahb, and Aman El Garhi. 2019. "Women, Irrigation, and Social Norms in Egypt: 'The More Things Change, the More They Stay the Same?'" *Water Policy* 21 (2): 291–309.

OECD (Organisation for Economic Co-operation and Development). 2022. *Tax Policy and Gender Equality: A Stocktake of Country Approaches.* Paris: OECD Publishing.

O'Sullivan, Michael. 2017. "Gender and Property Rights in Sub-Saharan Africa: A Review of Constraints and Effective Interventions." Policy Research Working Paper 8250, World Bank, Washington, DC.

Ouedraogo, Rasmane, and David Stenzel. 2021. "The Heavy Economic Toll of Gender-Based Violence: Evidence from Sub-Saharan Africa." IMF Working Paper WP/21/277, International Monetary Fund, Washington, DC.

Poyker, Michael. 2021. "Regime Stability and the Persistence of Traditional Practices." *Review of Economics and Statistics* (June 4, 2021): 1–45. http://www.poykerm.com/uploads/9/2/4/6/92466562/rs_poyker .pdf.

Ray, Isha. 2007. "Women, Water, and Development." *Annual Review of Environment and Resources* 32 (November): 421–49.

Rostiyanti, Susy F., Seng Hansen, and Steven Harison. 2020. "Understanding the Barriers to Women's Careers in Construction Industry: Indonesian Perspective." *International Journal of Construction Supply Chain Management* 10 (4): 267–83. doi: 10.14424/ijcscm100420-267-283.

Roy, Sanchari. 2019. "Discriminatory Laws against Women: A Survey of the Literature." Policy Research Working Paper 8719, World Bank, Washington, DC.

Ruhm, Christopher J. 1998. "The Economic Consequences of Parental Leave Mandates: Lessons from Europe." *Quarterly Journal of Economics* 113 (1): 285–317.

Sequeira, Aarón. 2022. "Eliminando dos arcaicas prohibiciones del Código de Trabajo para las mujeres [Eliminating two archaic Labor Code prohibitions for women]." *La Nación–Costa Rica,* January 19, 2022. https://www.pressreader.com/costa-rica/la-nacion-costa-rica/20220119/281646783510548.

Stotsky, Janet. 1997. "Gender Bias in Tax Systems," *Tax Notes International,* June 9, 1997: 1913–23.

Thurston, Rebecca C., Yue F. Chang, Karen Matthews, Roland von Känel, and Karestan Koenen. 2019. "Association of Sexual Harassment and Sexual Assault with Midlife Women's Mental and Physical Health." *JAMA Internal Medicine* 179 (1): 48–53. doi:10.1001/jamainternmed.2018.4886.

Torres, Jesica, Franklin Maduko, Isis Gaddis, Leonardo Iacovone, and Kathleen Beegle. 2021. "The Impact of the COVID-19 Pandemic on Women-Led Businesses." Policy Research Working Paper 9817, World Bank, Washington, DC.

Ubfal, Diego. 2022. "What Works in Supporting Women-Led Businesses?" Thematic Policy Brief for Gender Strategy Update, World Bank, Washington, DC.

UN (United Nations). 2022. "Dimensions and Examples of the Gender-Differentiated Impacts of Climate Change: The Role of Women as Agents of Change and Opportunities for Women." United Nations, Bonn. https://unfccc.int/sites/default/files/resource/sbi2022_07.pdf.

UNDESA (United Nations Department of Economic and Social Affairs). 2018. *UN Flagship Report on Disability and Sustainable Development Goals.* New York: United Nations.

van Koppen, Barbara. 2001. "Gender in Integrated Water Management: An Analysis of Variation." *Nature Resource Forum* 25 (4): 299–312.

Voena, Alessandra. 2015. "Yours, Mine, and Ours: Do Divorce Laws Affect the Intertemporal Behavior of Married Couples?" *American Economic Review* 105 (8): 2295–332. doi:10.1257/aer.20120234.

WHO (World Health Organization). 2018. "Global, Regional, and National Prevalence Estimates for Intimate Partner Violence against Women and Global and Regional Prevalence Estimates for Non-partner Sexual Violence against Women." WHO, Geneva.

World Bank. 2019a. "Brief on Violence against Women and Girls with Disabilities." World Bank, Washington, DC.

World Bank. 2019b. "Women in Water Utilities: Breaking Barriers." World Bank, Washington, DC.

World Bank. 2022a. "Afghanistan Welfare Monitoring Survey (AWMS)—Brief R2." World Bank, Washington, DC.

World Bank. 2022b. "Concept Note: Business Enabling Environment." Development Economics Global Indicators Group, World Bank, Washington, DC, December 2022. https://www.worldbank.org/content /dam/doingBusiness/pdf/BEE%20Concept%20Note_December%202022.pdf.

World Bank. 2022c. "Toward Available, Affordable, and Quality Childcare in East Asia and Pacific." World Bank, Washington, DC.

World Bank. 2022d. "Toward Available, Affordable, and Quality Childcare in Europe and Central Asia." World Bank, Washington, DC.

World Bank. 2022e. "Toward Available, Affordable, and Quality Childcare in Latin America and the Caribbean." World Bank, Washington, DC.

World Bank. 2022f. "Toward Available, Affordable, and Quality Childcare in the Middle East and North Africa." World Bank, Washington, DC.

World Bank. 2022g. "Toward Available, Affordable, and Quality Childcare in Sub-Saharan Africa." World Bank, Washington, DC.

World Bank. 2023. "Global Economic Prospects, January 2023." World Bank, Washington, DC. doi:10.1586/978-1-4648-1906-3.

World Bank and WHO (World Health Organization). 2011. *World Report on Disability*. Geneva: WHO.

Yount, Kathryn M., Yuk Fai Cheong, Zara Khan, Irina Bergenfeld, Nadaine Kaslow, and Cari Jo Clark. 2022. "Global Measurement of Intimate Partner Violence to Monitor Sustainable Development Goal 5." *BMC Public Health* 22: Art. 465. doi:10.1186/s12889-022-12822-9.

Zabalza, Antoni, and Zafiris Tzannatos. 1985. "The Effect of Britain's Anti-discriminatory Legislation on Relative Pay and Employment." *Economic Journal* 95 (379): 679–99. doi:10.2307/2233033.

Women, Business and the Law Indicator Scores

Women, Business and the Law presents indicator scores that offer objective and measurable benchmarks for global progress toward gender equality. Policy makers interested in improving equality of economic opportunity can look at their economy's scores on each indicator as a starting point for legal reform. Maps depict each economy's performance at the indicator level as of October 1, 2022.

MAP 1A.1 | *WOMEN, BUSINESS AND THE LAW* OVERALL SCORES

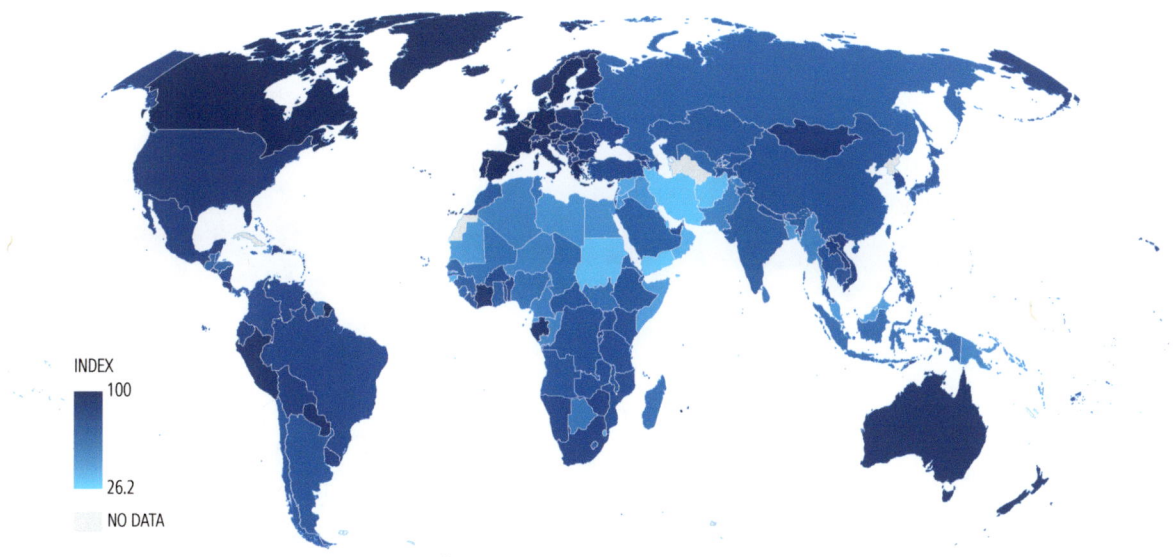

INDEX
100

26.2

NO DATA

IBRD 47032 | FEBRUARY 2023

Source: Women, Business and the Law database.

Mobility

MAP 1A.2 | *WOMEN, BUSINESS AND THE LAW* MOBILITY INDICATOR SCORES

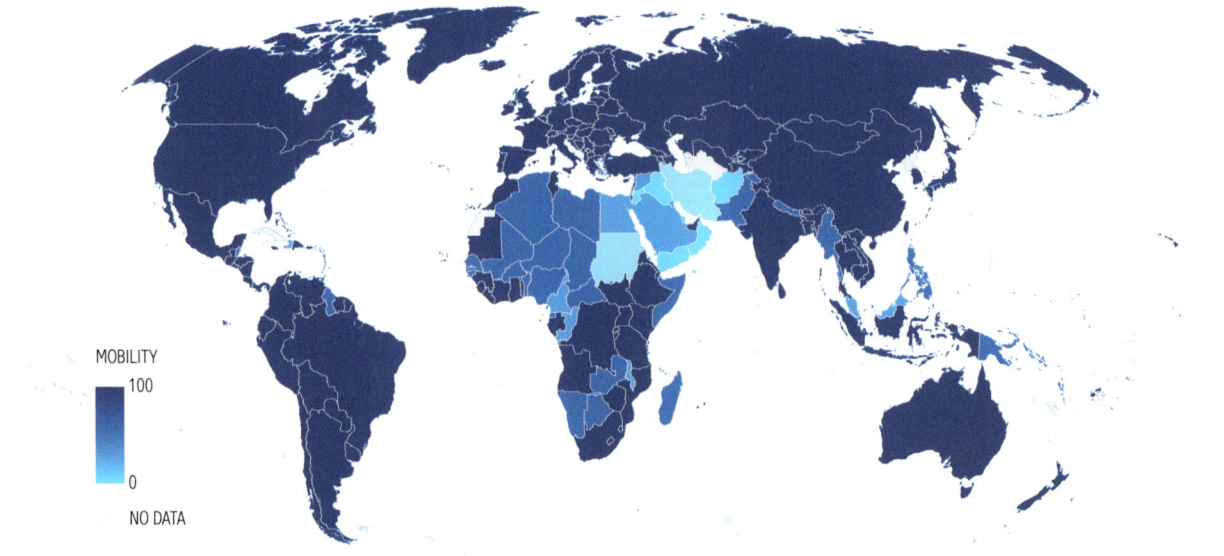

IBRD 47033 | FEBRUARY 2023

Source: Women, Business and the Law database.

Workplace

MAP 1A.3 | *WOMEN, BUSINESS AND THE LAW* WORKPLACE INDICATOR SCORES

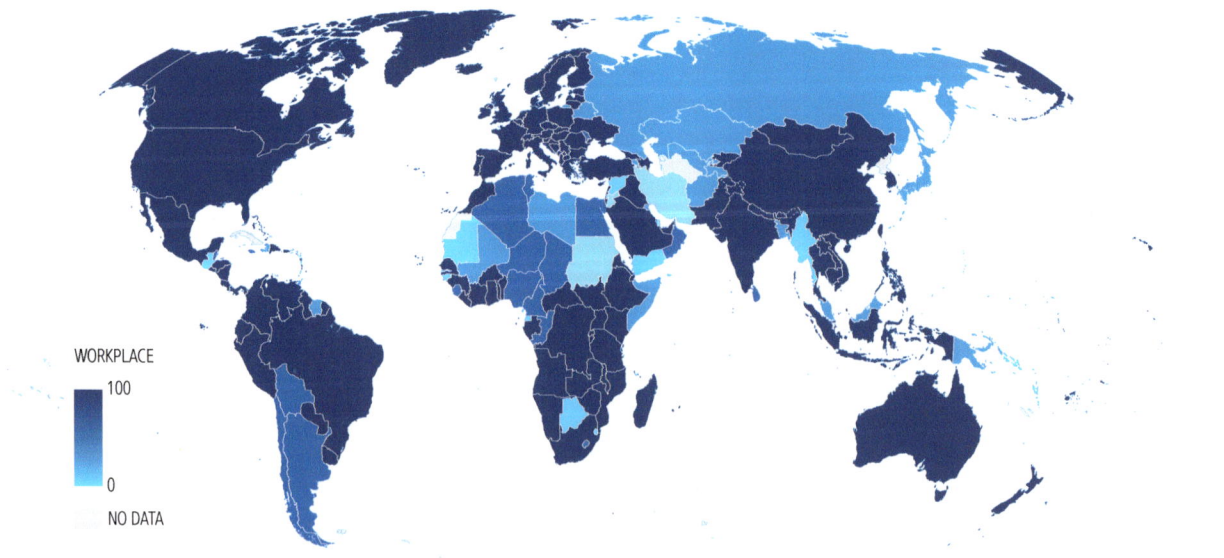

IBRD 47034 | FEBRUARY 2023

Source: Women, Business and the Law database.

Pay

MAP 1A.4 | *WOMEN, BUSINESS AND THE LAW* PAY INDICATOR SCORES

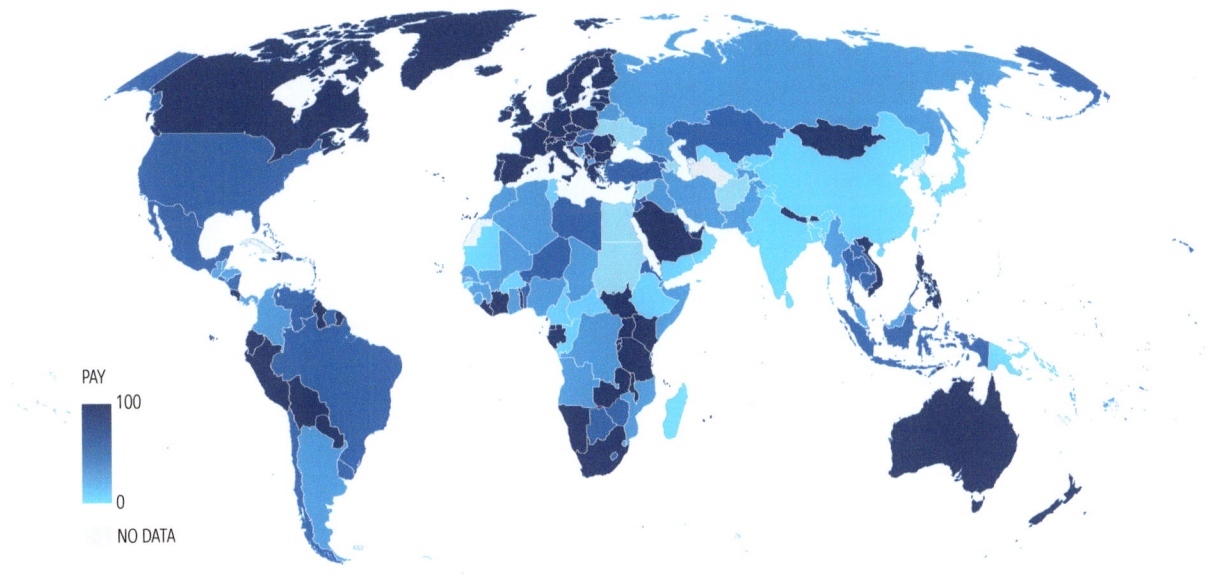

PAY
100

0

NO DATA

IBRD 47035 | FEBRUARY 2023

Source: Women, Business and the Law database.

Marriage

MAP 1A.5 | *WOMEN, BUSINESS AND THE LAW* MARRIAGE INDICATOR SCORES

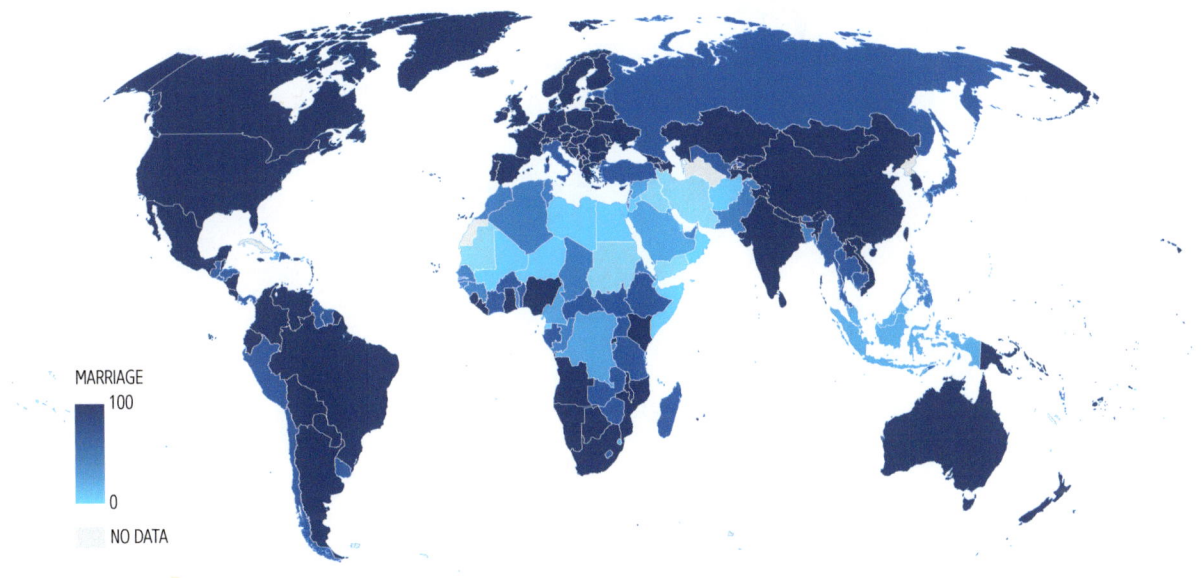

MARRIAGE
100

0

NO DATA

IBRD 47036 | FEBRUARY 2023

Source: Women, Business and the Law database.

Parenthood

MAP 1A.6 | *WOMEN, BUSINESS AND THE LAW* PARENTHOOD INDICATOR SCORES

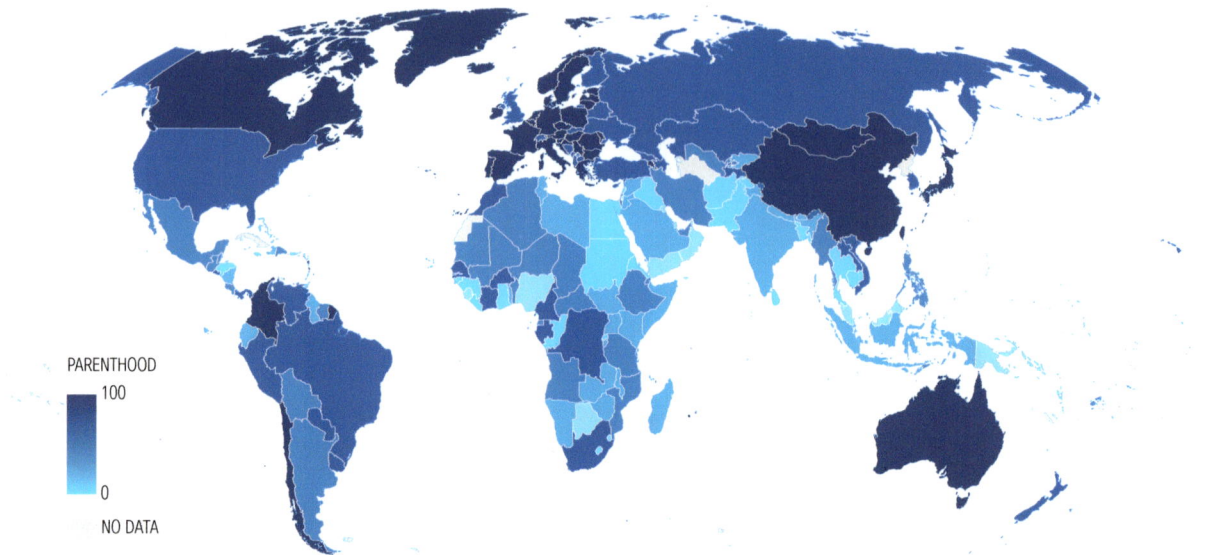

IBRD 47037 | FEBRUARY 2023

Source: Women, Business and the Law database.

Entrepreneurship

MAP 1A.7 | *WOMEN, BUSINESS AND THE LAW* ENTREPRENEURSHIP INDICATOR SCORES

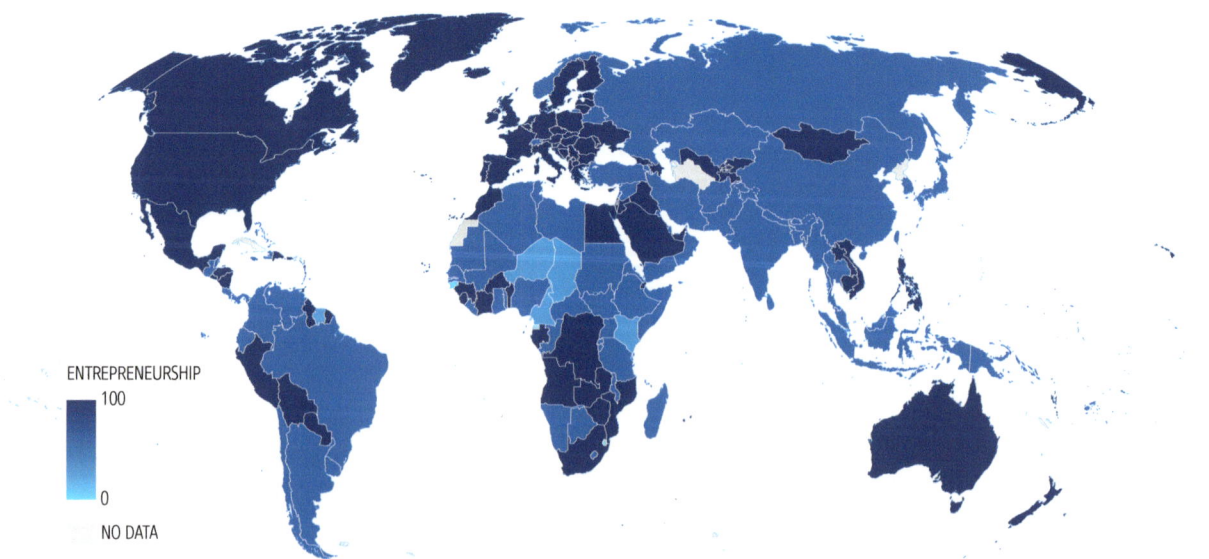

IBRD 47038 | FEBRUARY 2023

Source: Women, Business and the Law database.

🏠 Assets

MAP 1A.8 | *WOMEN, BUSINESS AND THE LAW* ASSETS INDICATOR SCORES

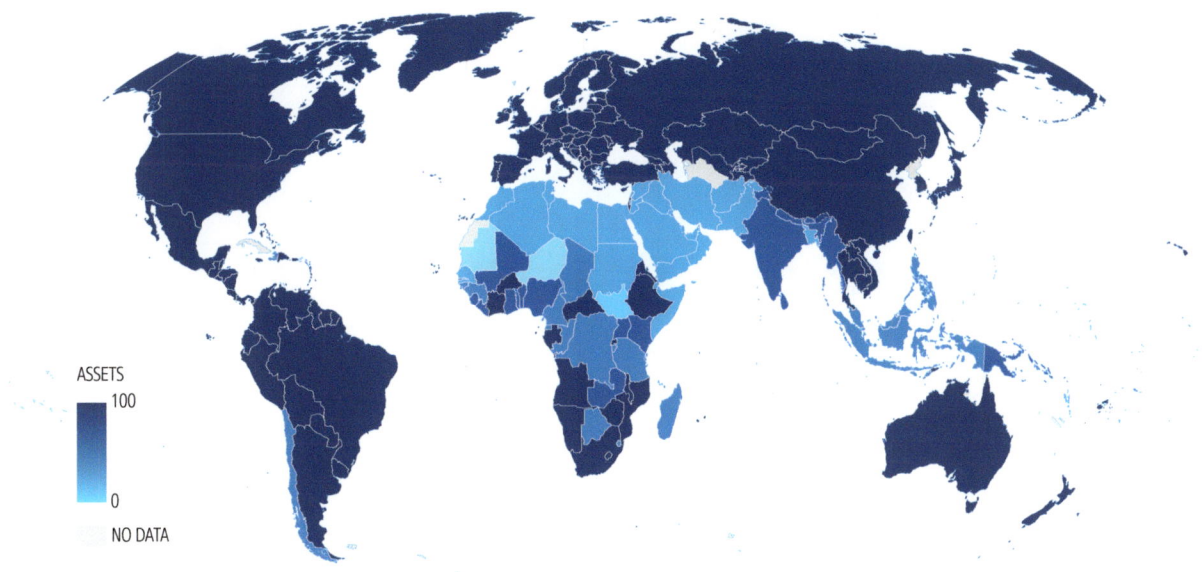

ASSETS
100
0
NO DATA

IBRD 47039 | FEBRUARY 2023

Source: Women, Business and the Law database.

👵 Pension

MAP 1A.9 | *WOMEN, BUSINESS AND THE LAW* PENSION INDICATOR SCORES

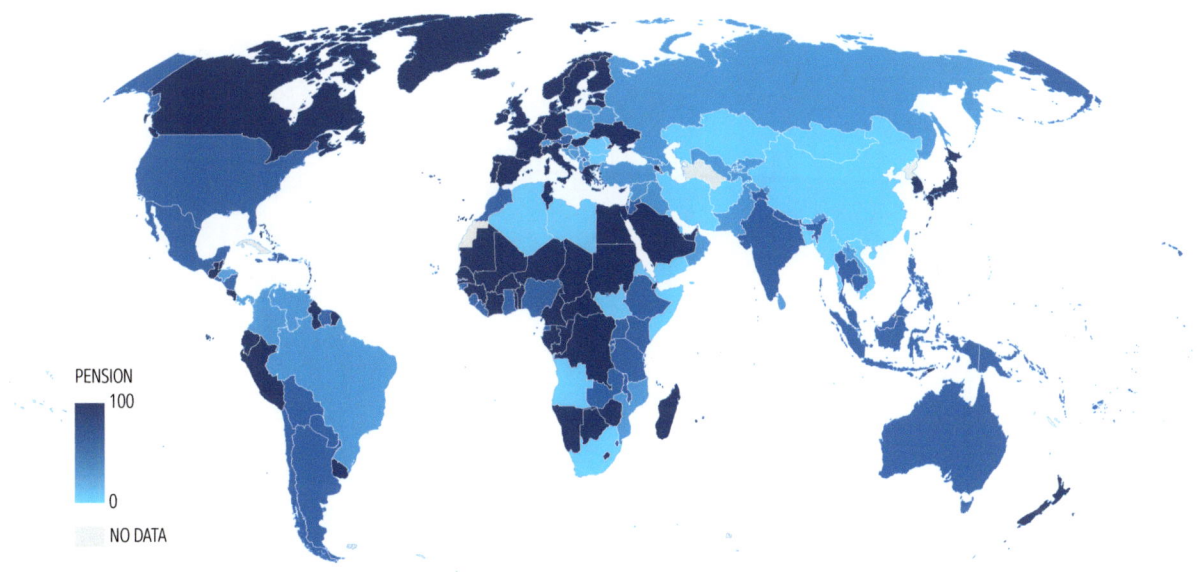

PENSION
100
0
NO DATA

IBRD 47040 | FEBRUARY 2023

Source: Women, Business and the Law database.

ANNEX 1B

Summaries of Reforms

From October 2, 2021, to October 1, 2022, *Women, Business and the Law* recorded 34 reforms aimed at improving gender equality in employment and entrepreneurial activity in 18 economies. Over the same period, two economies enacted five changes widening the legal gender gap.

✔ Reform increasing gender parity	✘ Reform decreasing gender parity

Afghanistan

✘ **Mobility**

The interim Taliban administration restricted women's right to travel outside the country in the same way as men.

✘ **Workplace**

The interim Taliban administration restricted women's right to get a job in the same way as men.

Bahrain

✔ **Pension**

Bahrain equalized the ages at which women and men can retire with full pension benefits.

Benin

✔ **Entrepreneurship**

Benin prohibited gender-based discrimination in financial services.

China

✔ **Parenthood**

China introduced paid parental leave.

Congo, Rep.

✔ **Workplace**

The Republic of Congo enacted legislation protecting women from sexual harassment in employment, including criminal penalties for such conduct.

✔ **Marriage**

The Republic of Congo enacted legislation protecting women from domestic violence.

Costa Rica

✔ **Pay**

Costa Rica removed restrictions on women's employment in jobs deemed dangerous.

✔ **Parenthood**

Costa Rica introduced paid paternity leave.

Côte d'Ivoire

✔ **Pay**

Côte d'Ivoire eliminated all restrictions on women's employment. Women can now work in industrial jobs and in jobs deemed dangerous in the same way as men.

✔ **Marriage**

Côte d'Ivoire enacted legislation protecting women from domestic violence.

✔ **Entrepreneurship**

Côte d'Ivoire prohibited gender-based discrimination in financial services.

Gabon

✔ **Mobility**

Gabon enacted legislation allowing women to apply for a passport in the same way as men.

✔ **Pay**

Gabon mandated equal remuneration for work of equal value. It also eliminated all restrictions on women's employment. Women can now work in industrial jobs and in jobs deemed dangerous in the same way as men.

Indonesia

✔ **Workplace**

Indonesia enacted legislation protecting women from sexual harassment in employment, including both criminal penalties and civil remedies for such conduct.

Iraq

✔ **Entrepreneurship**

Iraq prohibited gender-based discrimination in financial services.

Jamaica

✔ **Workplace**

Jamaica enacted legislation protecting women from sexual harassment in employment, including civil remedies for such conduct.

Kazakhstan

✔ **Pay**

Kazakhstan eliminated all restrictions on women's employment. Women can now work in industrial jobs and in jobs deemed dangerous in the same way as men.

Malawi

✔ **Parenthood**

Malawi introduced paid paternity leave.

Malta

✔ **Parenthood**

Malta introduced paid parental leave.

Mongolia

✔ **Pay**

Mongolia mandated equal remuneration for work of equal value.

✔ **Parenthood**

Mongolia introduced paid paternity leave.

Netherlands, The

✔ **Parenthood**

The Netherlands introduced paid parental leave.

Pakistan

✔ **Entrepreneurship**

Pakistan allowed women to register a business in the same way as men.

Saudi Arabia

✘ **Mobility**

Saudi Arabia restricted women's right to choose where to live and travel outside the country in the same way as men.

✘ **Marriage**

Saudi Arabia enacted legislation mandating women to obey their husbands.

Senegal

✔ **Pay**

Senegal removed restrictions on women's employment in industrial jobs.

✔ **Parenthood**

Senegal prohibited the dismissal of pregnant workers.

Uganda

✔ **Mobility**

Uganda granted women the same rights to choose where to live as men.

✔ **Assets**

Uganda equalized inheritance rights for both sons and daughters and male and female surviving spouses.

CHAPTER 2

Data Trends from Five Decades of Reform

Introduction

It is widely acknowledged that women's rights have expanded in recent decades. However, data verifying this improvement and exploring the path toward legal gender equality are generally limited by geography or time. The case of Belgium offers an interesting example. Belgium was the first economy to score 100 in the *Women, Business and the Law* index by passing an amendment to its law eliminating restrictions on women's employment in mining, which came into effect on May 10, 2010. Yet among the economies that today score 100, Belgium had one of the lowest scores in 1970. The *Women, Business and the Law* panel data set reveals Belgium's remarkable path to reach legal gender equality: reform stalled for a period of about 20 years, gained momentum at the end of the 1990s, and then progressed steadily for more than 10 years. The enactment of Law No. 3 of 1995 containing measures to promote women's employment and entrepreneurship, further amendments to the labor code in 1997, a royal decree introducing parental leave in 1999, and the adoption of measures to protect women from violence in 2003 all led to significant progress for gender equality, culminating with the adoption of a comprehensive Gender Act in 2007.

The legal implications of the women's rights movements of the 1960s and 1970s in the United States are well documented (for example, see Hazan, Weiss, and Zoabi 2021; Tertilt et al. 2022). However, there is minimal understanding of how, over time, laws have constrained women from obtaining equal rights and opportunities at the global level. The *Women, Business and the Law 2023* panel data thus fill an important gap in the available gender data. This chapter presents panel data for 190 economies for 53 years (1970–2022) and for 35 questions scored across the eight indicators in the *Women, Business and the Law* index. They are the first publicly available, comprehensive data that record women's legal rights across time and space for a large number of economies.[1] While the data set has been publicly available on the *Women, Business and the Law* website and has already been used by some researchers (see, for example, box 2.1), this report is the first to analyze the panel data comprehensively and to describe data trends from five decades of reform.

To construct the panel data set, *Women, Business and the Law* undertook meticulous data collection efforts to extend the data points back to 1970. This thorough historical analysis, which looked backward to seek and record each change in the law with regard to the 35 questions scored, reveals the course of moving toward legal gender equality from 1970 to 2022. Sources of historical laws included national libraries and archives, online repositories of laws across the world, and physical legal documents at the United States Library of Congress. This historical exercise also considered how the ability and freedom of economies to enact their own laws have changed over time. For example, economies that gained independence over the course of the historical panel were assigned the score of the economy of which they were part before their independence. For federal unions such as the former Yugoslavia and Soviet Union, unless there was a law at the national level of the constituent republics before independence (and there are several instances in which this was the case), the federal law was applied. For example, some economies of the former Soviet Union introduced their own labor codes, including Azerbaijan in 1971, Belarus in 1972, and Moldova in 1973. In these instances, the national labor codes are considered. A similar rationale was applied to formerly colonized economies, where national laws that generally applied during colonization were used as the legal basis. For the occasional instances in which missed historical reforms were brought to light, *Women, Business and the Law* revised the panel data to reflect the new information.

Now updated, the *Women, Business and the Law* panel data aim to empower rights holders, women's rights advocates, policy makers, and researchers alike to understand the geographic and temporal dimensions of the legal rights and barriers that women face.[2] Because the data set is broad in coverage, it facilitates analysis of when and where economies began removing legal gender barriers or advancing women's rights. More important, the data set enables users to track economies' progress (or regress) over time and outlines clearly where restrictions on women's rights and autonomy remain entrenched. For example, the panel data reveal that today women have just over three-quarters of the legal rights of men—in 1970, they had less than half. Although tangible progress has been made over the last decades, there is still a long way to go to reach gender parity in the law. In key areas of legal rights, women have been, and still are, worse off than men in the majority of economies around the world.

Users of the *Women, Business and the Law* panel data can draw lessons from the past to guide future decisions and identify priority areas for reform. Analysis of progress over time will also reveal important insights for overcoming bottlenecks in legal change, unlocking reform potential, and allowing researchers to improve their understanding of the conditions necessary for countries to reform. Such research can shed light on why certain rights were introduced at a given point in time and why women are still lacking rights in other areas.

Although removing barriers to gender equality in the law does not necessarily translate into proper implementation, especially in economies where social norms may disadvantage women or where state capacity to enforce the laws is limited, panel data like those presented by *Women, Business and the Law* are a crucial first step toward identifying key challenges and opportunities to accelerate progress. Laws codify and legitimize the status of women and girls within society, and they generally reflect societal attitudes toward women. As such, not only does the removal of legal barriers enhance women's rights per se, but also reforming gender-unequal laws has an important signaling and symbolic function as well as consequences for the economy and society at-large. A small group of reformers may spearhead legal change, which can trigger important societal debate and spark larger reform efforts, particularly if formerly taboo areas such as reproductive rights are touched (Macaulay 2002). Because legal barriers compound gender inequalities, understanding what works to remove them is pivotal for women seeking equal footing with men.

What are the benefits of legal gender reform?

Despite much progress, women today have only slightly over three-quarters of the economic rights of men as measured by *Women, Business and the Law*. Hence, many economies continue to uphold laws that restrict women's ability to hold property, become entrepreneurs, or make autonomous decisions in the public or private sphere. Working to close that gap is a key priority, as women's rights are beneficial not only for women themselves but also for societies at large. Overcoming persistent inequality is associated with better socioeconomic outcomes for women in a variety of areas such as human development, employment, and health (for a summary, see Roy 2019 and box 2.1).

Substantial research suggests many channels through which the benefits of legal equality extend beyond women themselves and spread to the broader economy. Removing legal constraints for women has been shown to be associated with various metrics of women's economic empowerment and socioeconomic development, including better labor market outcomes (Gonzales et al. 2015; Hyland, Djankov, and Goldberg 2020; Hyland and Islam 2021), better access to finance (Demirgüç-Kunt, Klapper, and

---

BOX 2.1 RECENT EVIDENCE LINKING *WOMEN, BUSINESS AND THE LAW* DATA TO BENEFICIAL SOCIOECONOMIC OUTCOMES

Since publication of the *Women, Business and the Law* panel data, researchers have increasingly used the data set to highlight the link between legal equality and women's economic outcomes. Some very recent additions to the literature include Sever (2022a), which finds that increasing legal gender equality boosts women's participation in the workforce and does not result in fewer men working. Lo Bue et al. (2022) highlight the overrepresentation of women among vulnerable workers and the correlation between legal discrimination against women and this particular gender gap.

Evidence is also growing that family leave policies, which are captured under the Parenthood indicator (figure B2.1.1, panel a), are correlated with women's empowerment. For example, Amin and Islam (2022) find a significant positive association between the legislated number of maternity leave days and female employment at the firm level. Furthermore, using evidence from *Women, Business and the Law*, Hyland and Shen (2022) show that closing the gap between the number of leave days allocated to mothers and to fathers is associated with a higher female labor force participation rate. Despite the growing evidence, assertations of causality are difficult to make given the potential for the female labor supply to influence government policies on parental leave. Furthermore, other factors, such as those related to the labor market and economic conditions more broadly, may affect both labor supply and leave policies, which the control variables do not perfectly capture.

(Box continues next page)

BOX 2.1 RECENT EVIDENCE LINKING *WOMEN, BUSINESS AND THE LAW* DATA TO BENEFICIAL SOCIOECONOMIC OUTCOMES *(continued)*

FIGURE B2.1.1 | MORE GENDER-EQUAL LAWS HAVE TANGIBLE BENEFITS FOR WOMEN

New evidence linking Women, Business and the Law *data with women's economic outcomes*

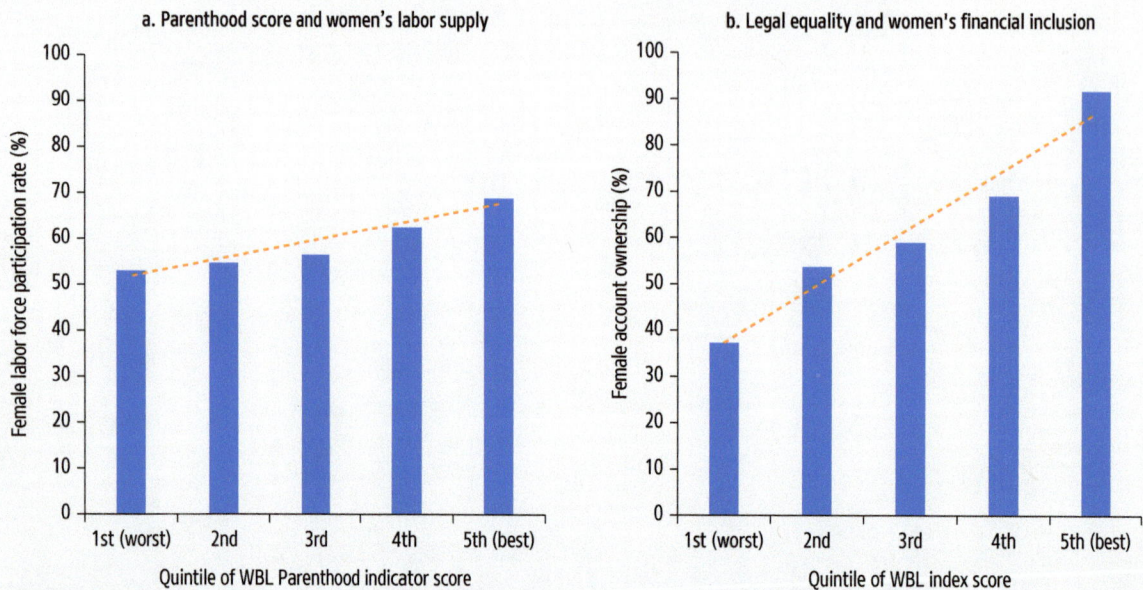

a. Parenthood score and women's labor supply

b. Legal equality and women's financial inclusion

Sources: Women, Business and the Law database. For panel a, World Bank, World Development Indicators database, https://databank.worldbank.org/source/world-development-indicators. For panel b, World Bank, Global Financial Inclusion (Findex), https://www.worldbank.org/en/publication/globalfindex.

Note: Panel a presents the correlation between the average *Women, Business and the Law* score within each quintile for the Parenthood indicator and the average female labor force participation rate for women ages 15–64 based on global data for 2019, according to modeled estimates from the International Labour Organization. Panel b presents the correlation between the average *Women, Business and the Law* score within each quintile and the average percentage of respondents who report having an account at a bank or another type of financial institution (including a mobile money account), using global data for 2021. Although both panels present a simple correlation, the relationship remains positive and statistically significant after controlling for income (measured as gross domestic product per capita provided in the World Bank's World Development Indicators database) and economy-level and time fixed effects.

Recent research also emphasizes the role of gender equality in boosting financial inclusion (Bertrand and Perrin 2022; Perrin and Hyland 2023). For example, Bertrand and Perrin (2022) find that legislation protecting women from discrimination in accessing credit is associated with a greater likelihood that a female entrepreneur will ask for credit when she needs it. However, the research finds no link between legal protections and the success rate of loan applications, highlighting the limitations of legal protections and the need for supporting policies to ensure implementation in practice. Perrin and Hyland (2023) find a positive association between legal gender equality and women's financial inclusion, which is summarized in figure B2.1.1, panel b. Claims to causality are also difficult to make in this instance, as women's financial inclusion may be influenced by developments in the macroeconomy and employment conditions, as well as by norms and values, which may be imperfectly captured by the control variables available.

Evidence that gender equality is important not just for women's economic empowerment but also for macroeconomic development is building as well. Sever (2022b) demonstrates how discriminatory laws constrain progress toward bridging cross-country differences in income, yielding tangible economic losses. Hence, removing legal barriers for women can help poorer economies to catch up with the living standards in richer economies (Sever 2022b). Similarly, other research has shown that legal inequalities prevent women from reaching their full economic potential, hampering economies' growth prospects (Christopherson et al. 2022). While such studies highlight the benefits of economic rights for economic development, the causality likely runs in both directions. Indeed, Tertilt et al. (2022) show that economic development is an important predictor of women's rights.

Singer 2013; Perrin and Hyland 2023), greater land and property ownership (Agarwal 2003; Deininger et al. 2021; Hallward-Driemeier, Hasan, and Rusu 2013), and better health outcomes (Anderson 2018; Harari 2019).

Specifically, removing barriers to women's ability to act autonomously and to work without legal limitations can help them to access better jobs and lead to higher workforce participation overall (Amin and Islam 2015; Htun, Jensenius, and Nelson-Nuñez 2019). Freedom from gender discriminatory laws can also help women to become entrepreneurs and access finance (Islam, Muzi, and Amin 2019). Furthermore, overcoming legal gender barriers can have positive implications for women's educational attainment (Branisa, Klasen, and Ziegler 2013; Deininger, Goyal, and Nagarajan 2013) and could potentially even lead to more investment in human capital (Deininger et al. 2019).

This growing body of evidence highlights the need to continue working to level the legal playing field between women and men. While gender equality matters as a development objective in its own right, it also serves as a means to ensure sustainable, long-run growth.

What motivates legal gender reform?

Although the knowledge base on gender-equal laws and their association with socioeconomic outcomes is steadily growing, there is limited systematic evidence explaining why economies decide to remove legal barriers for women in the first place. Insights into the motivations to eliminate discrimination are largely drawn from country-specific examples (see Braunmiller and Dry 2022; Geddes and Lueck 2002; Githae et al. 2022). Comparative evidence across economies is growing slowly. Data limitations may be one reason for limited comparative research on the drivers of legal gender reform. The *Women, Business and the Law* panel data can help to overcome this limitation.

Removing structural barriers that constrain women's participation in all spheres of public life requires an enabling environment and political will. A common driver for the expansion of women's rights is a country's political system. Democratic states are more often associated with an accelerated women's rights movement; they can facilitate reform and the expansion of women's rights, such as the right to vote (Lizzeri and Persico 2004). The extent to which various groups participate in the decision-making institutions of a democratic economy also matters. The absence of women from political life, for example, could lead to bias. In fact, greater female representation in a legislature seems to be an enabler for economies to pass more gender-sensitive laws, particularly in areas such as sexual harassment, rape, divorce, and domestic violence (Asiedu et al. 2018). Similarly, female leaders can have a significant effect on societies. They seem to do a better job of representing the needs of women (for an overview, see Duflo 2012). Indeed, research shows that female leadership is associated with enhanced gender equality in the legal system, an association that is stronger when women hold office for a longer period (Jung 2022). Also, a civil society that is actively challenging societal order or mobilizing societal action could create the momentum needed for governments to take action on discriminatory laws (Weldon 2002).

A look at the sequence in which economies have granted women rights offers insights into the factors underlying the decisions to expand those rights. For example, Doepke, Tertilt, and Voena (2012) find that different countries have followed distinct paths. Women in the United Kingdom and United States first gained basic economic rights, followed by political rights. Equal treatment in the labor market and greater control over their own bodies ultimately followed. By contrast, women in many African economies gained formal political rights as part of the end of colonialism and only later obtained economic rights (Doepke, Tertilt, and Voena 2012).

Education and higher human capital are also important enablers for increased gender equality in the law. Greater recognition of the importance of education can alter men's (and women's) preferences regarding women's rights. According to Doepke and Tertilt (2009), the expansion of married women's economic rights in the United Kingdom and United States throughout the nineteenth century can be attributed to technological change that increased the importance of human capital in the economy. Eastin and Prakash (2013) and Tertilt et al. (2022) also highlight the importance of economic development as a predictor of legal equality. Still, most of what is currently known about reform efforts stems from a limited set of economies (box 2.2).

BOX 2.2 DRIVERS, BARRIERS, AND MECHANISMS OF REFORMS: LESSONS FROM CASE STUDIES

Understanding the process underlying the enactment of legislative reforms to advance the rights of women is useful for economies interested in closing the legal gender gap. To this end, in 2022 *Women, Business and the Law* published seven case studies examining successful legal reforms aimed at gender equality in the Democratic Republic of Congo (Braunmiller and Dry 2022), Ethiopia (Alemayehu et al., forthcoming), India (Braunmiller et al., forthcoming), Kenya (Githae et al. 2022), São Tomé and Príncipe (Mazoni and Corminales 2022), South Africa (Arekapudi and Mazoni 2022), and Togo (Affoum and Dry 2022). And the World Bank's Global Business Regulation published a case study on reforms toward gender equality recently implemented in the United Arab Emirates (World Bank 2022). These case studies provide lessons on how to pursue gender equality reforms.

The activism of women's groups, for example, has often proved instrumental in the reform process. Gender champions across local civil society groups and sustained political will and momentum for the women's rights movement have been an active force behind historic reforms, including the gradual eradication of marital power in South Africa, with the Matrimonial Property Act in 1984, its amendment in 1988, and the General Law Fourth Amendment in 1993, and in the Democratic Republic of Congo, with the adoption of the Congolese Law on Parity and amendments to the civil code in 2015–16. Reforms in both the Democratic Republic of Congo and South Africa removed significant restrictions, allowing women to sign contracts, start jobs, and register businesses without their husbands' authorization. In India, a thriving civil society also contributed to identifying gaps, drafting legislation, and organizing public opinion through campaigns, discussions, and protests, leading to enactment of the 2005 Domestic Violence Act.

Strategic multistakeholder coalitions bringing together government, civil society organizations, and the international community have also successfully pursued important reforms. In São Tomé and Príncipe, decades of advocacy led by trailblazing women activists, support from gender champions at the highest levels of government, and legislative drafting assistance from international counterparts pushed the issue of pervasive domestic violence to the top of the economy's legislative agenda, leading to the enactment of the 2008 Maria das Neves Law. In Togo, a multistakeholder effort by local civil society organizations, the government, and international organizations played a key role in reforming the Persons and Family Code in 2012 and 2014, allowing women to choose where to live and work, and to head a household with no restrictions. In Ethiopia, tripartite negotiations among the Confederation of Trade Unions, Employers' Association, and the government led to labor reforms in 2019, which lengthened paid maternity leave and introduced paid paternity leave.

Research and data highlighting inequalities and the cost of inaction have additionally served as compelling support for reform. In Kenya, research on the poor working conditions of women, including unfair compensation and sexual harassment, guided the development of historic labor reforms in 2007 that granted equal rights and protections for women. Similarly, advocates used data on the pervasiveness and economic costs of gender-based violence during the parliamentary deliberations leading

(Box continues next page)

BOX 2.2 DRIVERS, BARRIERS, AND MECHANISMS OF REFORMS: LESSONS FROM CASE STUDIES *(continued)*

to the adoption of the Protection against Domestic Violence Act in 2015. In the Democratic Republic of Congo, advocates leveraged the economic case for gender equality, linking legal constraints to practical barriers for entrepreneurs, to convince skeptics that legal reform was an economic necessity. In Togo, activists used compelling sociological data to demonstrate that the discriminatory family law no longer reflected the reality of Togolese society. In the United Arab Emirates, *Women, Business and the Law* data have been instrumental in identifying gaps in existing legislation and informing a package of comprehensive reforms toward gender equality. These reforms included the 2020 amendments of the Personal Status Law, affecting women's freedom of movement and removing the duty of obedience, and the Federal Labor Law, mandating equal remuneration for work of equal value.

International commitments under the Convention on the Elimination of All Forms of Discrimination against Women and technical assistance from international partners, including the African Development Bank, International Labour Organization, and World Bank, played an important role in bringing about these reforms.

The path toward legal reform has not always been linear or smooth, though. In some cases, the enactment of legislation was stalled for years—sometimes decades—and was the result of intense debates and negotiations. For instance, in Togo, civil society started denouncing the inequalities contained in the Persons and Family Code in the late 1980s. However, following violent incidents in response to protests advocating democracy and political pluralism from 1990 to 1993, the ties between Togo and the international community were cut for 15 years. As a result, the process of reform was stalled for almost two decades. When dialogue and diplomacy slowly resumed in 2008, so did the reform movement, with the historic reforms of the Persons and Family Code in 2012 and 2014. Similarly, India's journey of social and legal reforms to address domestic violence followed a unique path spanning nearly five decades of debates, starting from addressing dowry-related violence, then recognizing additional offenses in the criminal law, and finally enacting the Protection of Women from Domestic Violence Act in 2005, which for the first time accorded protective rights and welfare measures to survivors. Likewise, the Kenya Protection against Domestic Violence Bill of 2015 was the culmination of more than 20 years of research, advocacy, and lobbying by Kenyan civil society organizations as well as a significant achievement for Kenyan parliamentarians.

Together, these lessons can provide important insights for policy makers, advocates, and international organizations pursuing legal gender equality.

Information on the drivers of legal reform across a more diverse set of economies has been largely absent. However, this void was recently filled by Tertilt et al. (2022), who undertake a comparative assessment of how gender discriminatory laws are reformed. The authors use the *Women, Business and the Law* panel data set and supplement it with information on political rights (such as suffrage and the right to stand for election) and body rights (such as the right to an abortion and access to contraception) to build a data set covering four areas—economic rights, political rights, labor rights, and rights over one's own body. They develop a political economy model outlining four important economic channels through which reform can happen: (1) the bargaining power channel (rights can affect how resources are shared within households); (2) the parental altruism channel (women's rights can affect men through the impacts on their daughters and increased investment in children); (3) the income channel (more rights for women can increase household resources); and (4) the public policy channel (including women in policy making can affect policy formation). The authors find that, overall, women's rights are strongly associated with economic development. Of these channels, their results suggest that the income channel is an important driver of the expansion of women's rights, particularly economic and labor rights. Tertilt et al. (2022) also find that parental altruism is an important channel through which women's rights increase over time.

Although many factors beyond legal reform benefit women's economic empowerment and broader development outcomes, legal reforms are actionable and, in contrast to changing norms and attitudes, achievable in the short run (Hyland, Djankov, and Goldberg 2020). However, how to achieve legal reform and what enabling factors need to be in place for laws to be implemented successfully have received limited attention. Shedding more light on what factors are successful in driving reforms can guide future policy and accelerate movement down the path toward legal gender equality.

Unpacking reform efforts: Main takeaways

For decades, economies have reformed existing laws or introduced new legislation to provide women with more legal rights. This section presents five main takeaways from the *Women, Business and the Law* panel data that describe patterns of reform, including how, where, and how fast laws have changed since 1970. In doing so, it highlights the remarkable catch-up effect that some economies have exhibited, while also stressing that more work lies ahead to reach gender parity in the law.

Takeaway 1. In the last five decades, the global average of the Women, Business and the Law *score has improved by about two-thirds as a result of more than 2,000 reforms expanding women's legal rights.*

Over the course of 53 years (1970–2022) and in the 35 areas measured, economies have introduced a staggering 2,151 reforms, improving the average *Women, Business and the Law* score from 45.8 in 1970 to 77.1 today.[3] However, another 1,549 reforms will be needed to reach legal gender equality everywhere.

Counting the positive changes in the law—reforms—that have occurred since 1970, the data show that those reforms have not been distributed equally across the decades. The 1970s and the 1980s saw a similar rate of change, with 279 and 259 reforms, respectively. The year 1990 kick-started two decades of increased reform. In the 1990s, 433 reforms were introduced, followed by the introduction of a striking 611 reforms in the 2000s. Since then, the progress of reform has slowed: only 447 reforms were implemented from 2010 to 2019 (figure 2.1), with a spike of 63 reforms in 2019—one of the highest number of reforms overall per year. Since 2020, economies have enacted 122 reforms. The annual rate of reform has fallen since, and 2022 saw the smallest number of reforms since 2001. While some natural slowdown of reforms can be expected as economies progress to more gender-equal laws, this slowdown could become a concern if competing priorities are taking attention away from legislative reforms to achieve gender equality.

In the 1970s, many economies addressed the lower-hanging fruit and updated legal provisions that once limited the basic agency and freedom of movement of women and girls. For example, in 1970 Ecuador updated its 1857 civil code, removing restrictions for married women. The new civil code enabled a married woman to sign a legally binding contract, register a business, go to work, administer property, and open a bank account without the consent of her husband. Similarly, Ghana and Kenya enacted new laws in the 1970s allowing women to choose where to live.

FIGURE 2.1 | MORE THAN 2,000 REFORMS HAVE BEEN IMPLEMENTED SINCE 1970, MAKING IMPRESSIVE PROGRESS TOWARD MORE GENDER-EQUAL LAWS

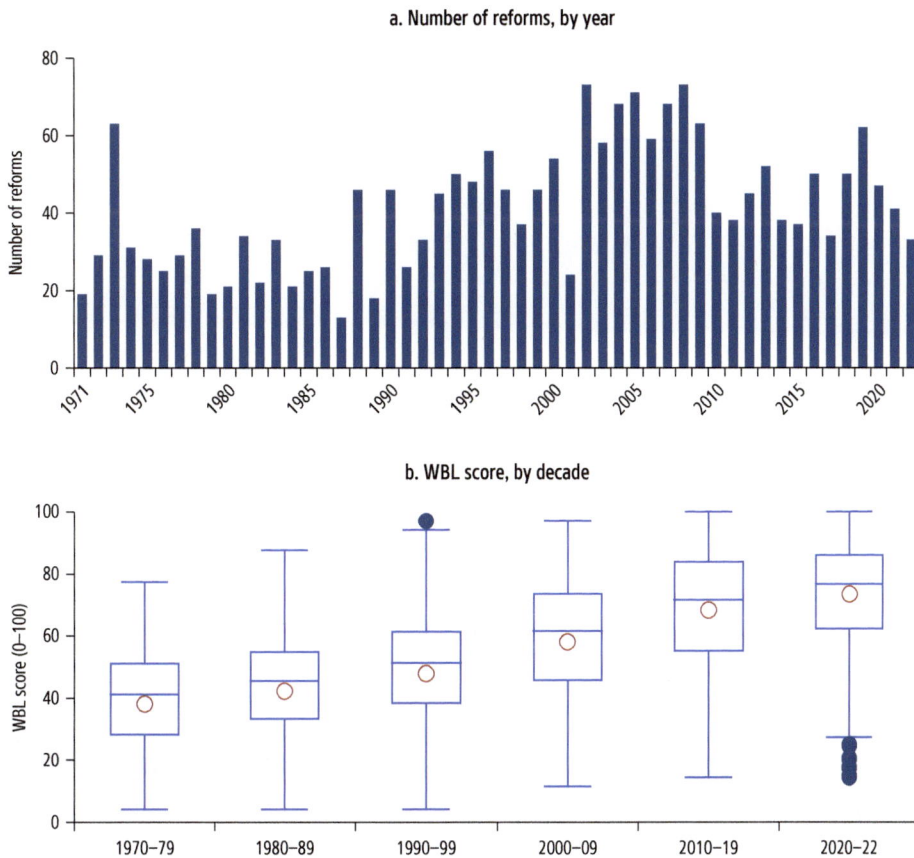

a. Number of reforms, by year

b. WBL score, by decade

Source: Women, Business and the Law database.
Note: Panel a shows the number of reforms, by year, that have removed legal gender barriers for the 190 economies in the *Women, Business and the Law* data set. A reform is counted if, within any of the 35 areas of measurement, an answer changes from "no" to "yes" because of the adoption of a new law or the amendment of an existing law. Panel b shows how the number of reforms affects the overall *Women, Business and the Law* score, by decade. The "box and whiskers" plot shows the distribution of the *Women, Business and the Law* score by decade. The "box" plots the interquartile range, showing the first and third quartile, with the median in between. The "whiskers" show the range from the minimum to the maximum values. The circle denotes the mean of the *Women, Business and the Law* score. The blue dots outside the "whiskers" denote outliers. An outlier is an economy outside 1.5 times the interquartile range.

More important, these decades were also marked by the introduction of novel legislation in the areas of Parenthood and Pension. In the 1970s, 25 economies expanded legislation by making it illegal for employers to dismiss pregnant workers. Among the regions, Europe and Central Asia as well as the Organization for Economic Co-operation and Development (OECD) high-income economies were the first to adopt legislation prohibiting the dismissal of pregnant workers. Other regions soon followed suit. In Sub-Saharan Africa, Somalia was the first economy to issue legislation protecting women from dismissal by an employer during pregnancy.[4] In Latin America and the Caribbean, 14 economies already had such legislation in place. In 1974, Argentina, hitherto lacking such legislation, was the first to institute a reform.[5]

Similarly, in the 1970s, 20 economies promoted reforms either to introduce old-age pension systems for the first time or to update existing ones, allowing women and men to retire equally with full benefits. These reforms also affected women's ability to retire with partial pension benefits. In six economies, the new or amended laws set equal ages at which women and men can retire with partial pension benefits, whereas in 14 economies, the legislation did not establish the possibility for retirement with partial benefits. Reform efforts in this area began in Latin America and the Caribbean and in Sub-Saharan Africa; soon after, other regions followed suit. In 1972, Samoa introduced the National Provident Fund Act 1972 and became the first economy in the East Asia and Pacific region to reform in this area. In 1974, Tunisia became the first economy in the Middle East and North Africa region to introduce an old-age pension system that set equal ages for women and men to retire with full pension benefits.

The introduction of new laws in the 1970s and 1980s quickened the pace of reform in the 1990s and 2000s, albeit in different areas. In the 1990s, many economies introduced pioneering new legislation in areas such as nondiscrimination in employment and protection of women from sexual harassment in the workplace. Since the turn of the century, economies have substantially increased their efforts to reform their laws to reach legal gender parity in all aspects of a woman's working life. Between 2000 and 2009, more than 600 reforms were introduced, with a peak of 73 reforms in 2002 and 2008.

However, since that peak, the removal of legal barriers has slowed. While reform efforts may naturally slow down as economies become more gender equal in their laws, several economies have not moved in years. For instance, six economies have implemented several reforms in the past and have, therefore, surpassed the global average score in the *Women, Business and the Law* index, but they have not implemented any reforms for the last 15 years in the areas measured. These six economies are The Bahamas, Guyana, Romania, St. Lucia, Tanzania, and Zimbabwe. Tanzania undertook an impressive reform effort in the 2000s, but since 2006 has had a stagnant score of 81.3, with room for improvement in all areas except Mobility, Workplace, and Pay. A similar pattern is observable for Guyana. Guyana significantly reformed before the turn of the century, with an increase in score from 66.3 to 86.9. Then, the economy's reform efforts came to a halt, with room for improvement in Mobility, Marriage, and Parenthood. Romania stands out because its reform efforts took off only around the turn of the century, improving from a score of 65 in 2000 to 90.6 in 2008—a steep increase in a short period of time. Since then, however, Romania has not implemented any reforms and still has a comparably low score in the area of Pension. More research is needed to understand why.

In 2022, only 34 reforms were recorded, a historic low since 2001. This low level of reform, however, does not imply that reforming gender-unequal laws has been pushed off the agenda in all economies. Several key reform bills are currently stalled in parliamentary deadlock. For example, a marriage bill in Bhutan has been pending since 2016. Burundi has been working on a new inheritance law since 2004. Nigeria introduced a gender and equal opportunity bill to the Senate in March 2016 and then again in 2019, but it has suffered several setbacks in the legislative chambers. Economies are still pushing for more gender-equal laws, but many underlying reasons, including patriarchal cultural norms, opposition from religious groups, and political instability, are hampering their legislative efforts.

Yet there is also cause for optimism. In 2022, after years of delay, Uganda passed the long-awaited Succession (Amendment) Act, addressing the inequality and marginalization of women and girls after the death of a spouse by equalizing inheritance rights between both genders. The act also allows married women to choose where to live without having to acquire the domicile of their husbands. Furthermore, Sierra Leone passed the Gender Empowerment Act in November 2022 after several setbacks. The president signed the bill into law in January 2023. While passed after the cut-off date for this year's report, the new legislation manifests Sierra Leone's commitment to legal reform. In September 2022, Sierra Leone also passed the Customary Land Rights Act, boosting the rights of rural landowners and women. Despite some recent examples of how political will and momentum can lead to tangible progress, there is still a long way to go to reach gender parity in the law for all women everywhere.

Takeaway 2. Only 14 economies have achieved legal gender parity in 2022, as measured by Women, Business and the Law, and progress has been uneven across regions and over time.

Despite the significant increase in the average *Women, Business and the Law* score over time, to date only 14 economies—all OECD high income—score 100. Thus 176 economies still have room to improve, and at the recent pace of reform they will need at least another 50 years to reach 100. This means that a young woman entering the workforce today will retire before she is able to enjoy gender-equal rights during her working life.

A score of 100 represents equal rights and opportunities for men and women in all 35 areas of measurement. This score can be interpreted as the absence of legal inequality for a woman throughout her working life in the areas covered by the index. While other rights are certainly important, these 35 areas represent the minimum set of rights that must be in place for a woman to have economic opportunities equal to those of a man throughout her adult working life. Ongoing developments by the *Women, Business and the Law* project to add new indicators and data points as well as to assess implementation of the law in practice will provide a more comprehensive measure of legal equality.

By enacting an amendment in May 2010 that removed restrictions on women's employment in mining, Belgium was the first economy to reach gender parity in the law. For the previous 40 years, since the earliest period covered by *Women, Business and the Law*, none of the economies included in the index had reached legal gender parity. There has been plenty of progress, but only within the last decade and only in some high-income economies have women made far-reaching progress in gaining legal equality as workers, spouses, consumers, or entrepreneurs. While it took until 2010 for the first economy to reach full gender equality in the law, by 2022, 44 economies had closed most gender gaps in the law, reaching a score of 90 or higher in the *Women, Business and the Law* index. Canada, for example, was the first economy to reach that intermediary milestone in 1990 (scoring 95). Yet Canada did not achieve full gender parity for almost two more decades. In 2019, Canada eventually earned a score of 100 by introducing a new law that reserves 35 days of paid parental leave for the father.[6] The 14 economies that have, by now, reached gender parity in the law are Belgium, Canada, Denmark, France, Germany, Greece, Iceland, Ireland, Latvia, Luxembourg, the Netherlands, Portugal, Spain, and Sweden.

Similarly, the lower tier of the index (economies scoring 25 and below) remained sticky for a long time. In 1970, 12 economies scored 25 or below in the *Women, Business and the Law* index, indicating that women had only a quarter of the legal rights of men.[7] This number gradually fell to 0, with the Republic of Yemen being the last economy to exit the lowest tier of the index. In 2008, the Republic of Yemen amended its labor code, equalizing women and men before the law in terms of mandatory retirement, rising to a score of 26.9 in the *Women, Business and the Law* index, the same score as today.[8]

Even though some economies began the reform process only within the last two decades, *Women, Business and the Law* panel data show that reforming the law is, in fact, a global phenomenon. Worldwide, every economy has implemented at least one reform since 1970, allowing women to inch closer to equal economic opportunity under the law. Also, since the 2000s, the pace of reform has accelerated in regions that were rather slow to reform in the previous decades, such as South Asia (out of a total of 66 reforms, 54 were implemented since 2000) or East Asia and Pacific (out of a total of 222 reforms, 138 were implemented since 2000). Overall, 1,180 reforms have been implemented since the turn of the century. Thus, since 2000, economies have implemented, on average, 51 reforms a year, compared to 33 reforms a year before 2000. Although this finding is encouraging, it is not enough. Reform efforts toward gender parity need to be accelerated and prioritized.

Meanwhile, despite the progress made, gender disparities persist at the regional and income levels. Today, equality of economic opportunity across genders is highest in OECD high-income economies, where the average score in the *Women, Business and the Law* index is 95.3 points, and lowest in the Middle East and North Africa region, where the average score is 53.2 points.

OECD high-income economies have reached today's score through continual reform efforts over decades. In 1970, women in these economies faced multiple legal barriers, reflected by a rather low average score of 55.2. This score is comparable to the average score of the Middle East and North Africa region today (53.2). By implementing 490 reforms over the last 52 years, OECD high-income economies have been able to advance in the *Women, Business and the Law* index by about 40 points. Spain is the region's top-reforming economy, implementing 23 reforms between 1970 and 2022, followed by Austria, Luxembourg, and Portugal, each with 21 reforms. Among the OECD high-income economies, Japan implemented the fewest reforms (6), and scores lowest in the OECD high-income cohort as of 2022 (78.75).

There are also regional differences in the timing of reform efforts (figure 2.2). Many economies in Latin America and the Caribbean, likely influenced by early movements toward reform in Europe (Htun and Weldon 2011), began their reform process in the 1970s, reaching their peak in the 1990s, when the region enacted 107 reforms. In 1981, Suriname alone instituted 10 reforms. By contrast, most other regions reached their reform peak in the 2000s: Sub-Saharan Africa, with 169 reforms; OECD high-income economies, with 143 reforms; and Europe and Central Asia, with 109 reforms.

The significant spike in reforms among Sub-Saharan African economies in the 2000s may also be linked to the adoption of the Protocol to the African Charter on Human and Peoples' Rights on the Rights of Women in Africa (Maputo Protocol) by the African Union in 2003. The protocol, which entered into force in 2005 and has been ratified by 42 of the 55 member states of the African Union, guarantees expansive rights to African women and girls and includes 30 of the 35 areas measured

FIGURE 2.2 | PROGRESS TOWARD GENDER-EQUAL LAWS HAS BEEN UNEVEN ACROSS TIME AND REGIONS

Number of women's rights reforms implemented, by decade and region

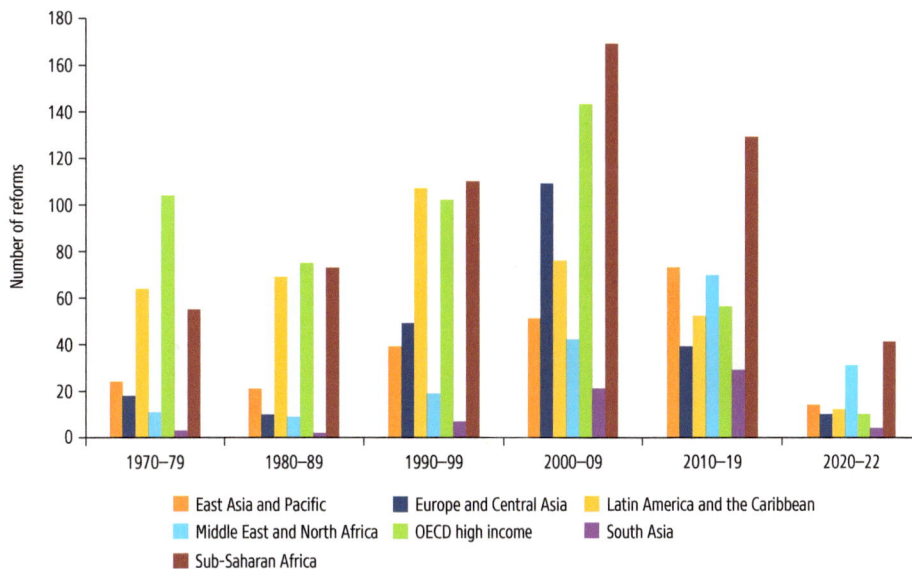

Source: *Women, Business and the Law* database.
Note: The figure shows the number of reforms, by region, that removed legal gender barriers. A reform is counted if, within any of the 35 areas of measurement, an answer changes from "no" to "yes" because of the adoption of a new law or the amendment of an existing law. The last set of bars reflects reforms enacted for only three years: 2020, 2021, and 2022. All regions are classified as of 2022. OECD = Organisation for Economic Co-operation and Development.

by *Women, Business and the Law*. During the 2000s, the *Women, Business and the Law* score increased in 17 economies in Sub-Saharan Africa due to the introduction of legislation on sexual harassment in employment. For some of them, the Maputo Protocol was a key driver.[9] Benin, for example, enacted the Law to Repress Sexual Harassment and Protect Victims, which defines sexual harassment and criminalizes such conduct in the context of employment. Namibia incorporated the prohibition of discrimination and sexual harassment in employment in its Labor Act of 2007, which entitles employees to civil remedies after their unfair dismissal as a result of sexual harassment. Similarly, Rwanda's Law on Prevention and Punishment of Gender-Based Violence establishes imprisonment and fines for any person guilty of sexual harassment in the workplace. Victims affected by this type of violence have the right to claim damages.

Since the early 2000s, South Asia's reforms have also taken off, with Nepal standing out by granting spouses equal rights to immovable property in 2002, allowing women to be head of household in 2008, enacting legislation to protect women from domestic violence in 2009 and from sexual harassment in employment in 2015, and enacting several amendments and laws that enhanced women's legal rights related to inheritance, divorce, and employment in 2018.[10]

In Europe and Central Asia, most reforms were undertaken in the 2000s across all economies (109 reforms). In the aftermath of the collapse of the Soviet Union, the initial focus of the newly independent republics was on the development of stable political and economic systems along with independent cultural identities separate from the decades of Soviet rule. Hence, legislating and enforcing gender equality were not an immediate priority for state officials, contributing to the reemergence of stereotypes about gender roles in the early 1990s (Wolchik 1995). By the same token, in 1990, Europe and Central Asia had a comparatively higher score (60.2) in the *Women, Business and the Law* index than other regions (East Asia and Pacific, 53.2; Sub-Saharan Africa 46.3; South Asia, 43.7; Middle East and North Africa, 32.7). This relatively high score could be attributed to the fact that the Soviet Union was known to have solid policies that allowed women to balance their roles as mothers and labor force participants. For example, a strong social welfare net consisting of state-sponsored childcare, food subsidies, communal dining halls, and health care was established to allow women to participate in the labor force and education system (Goldman 1993; Lapidus 1978).

The Middle East and North Africa's reform efforts took off only in the 2010s. In the last 13 years (2010–22), the region implemented more reforms (100) than in the previous four decades combined (81 reforms from 1970 to 2009). In the first three decades covered by the *Women, Business and the Law* panel data, reform efforts in the Middle East and North Africa region were concentrated mainly in the areas of Parenthood and Pension. Despite a current score of 43 on the Assets indicator, by far the lowest across all regions, only one economy in the Middle East and North Africa has undertaken reform efforts since 1970. In 1993, Malta enacted a law granting spouses equal authority to administer assets during marriage and equal rights to immovable property.[11] These fundamental rights are codified in civil codes, personal status laws, or family codes and expressed in judicial decisions. Expanding women's rights in these areas might be slower and politically more contentious in regions where reform efforts are often framed as a matter of national, religious, or cultural identity (Shachar 2001). Economies might claim that family law reform touches on the status of religion, culture, or kinship and may resist reform efforts to maintain the status quo in these areas (Htun and Weldon 2015; Kang 2015; Moustafa 2013).

Within regions, some economies have made much more progress than others. Altogether, the regions' top-reforming economies are, in OECD high income, Spain (23 reforms); in the Middle East and North Africa region, Malta and the United Arab Emirates (22 reforms each); in Sub-Saharan Africa, São Tomé and Príncipe and South Africa (22 reforms each); in East Asia and Pacific, the Lao People's Democratic Republic (21 reforms); in Latin America and the Caribbean, Bolivia and Brazil (20 reforms each); in South Asia, Nepal (16 reforms); and in Europe and Central Asia, Georgia and Türkiye (13 reforms each). All of these economies are well ahead of their regional peers. On average, economies in these regions reformed as follows: OECD high income (14 reforms), Middle East and North Africa (9 reforms), East Asia and Pacific (9 reforms), Latin America and the Caribbean (12 reforms), South Asia (8 reforms), and Europe and Central Asia (10 reforms).

Compared with the regional variation, differences in reform efforts have been less pronounced across income groups (figure 2.3). Instead, reforming economies' laws to provide better opportunities for women has followed a relatively consistent pattern across income groups. High-income economies have implemented a total of 742 reforms, with economies implementing between 1 (Qatar) and 23 (Spain) reforms. Upper-middle-income economies[12] have implemented 573 reforms, with a spread of between 1 (Palau) and 22 (South Africa) reforms. Lower-middle-income economies have implemented a total of 559 reforms, with a spread of between 1 (the Federated States of Micronesia) and 22 (São Tomé and Príncipe) reforms. Finally, low-income economies

FIGURE 2.3 | IMPLEMENTING GENDER REFORM IS NOT DEPENDENT ON INCOME LEVEL

Number of women's rights reforms implemented per economy, by income level, 1970–2022

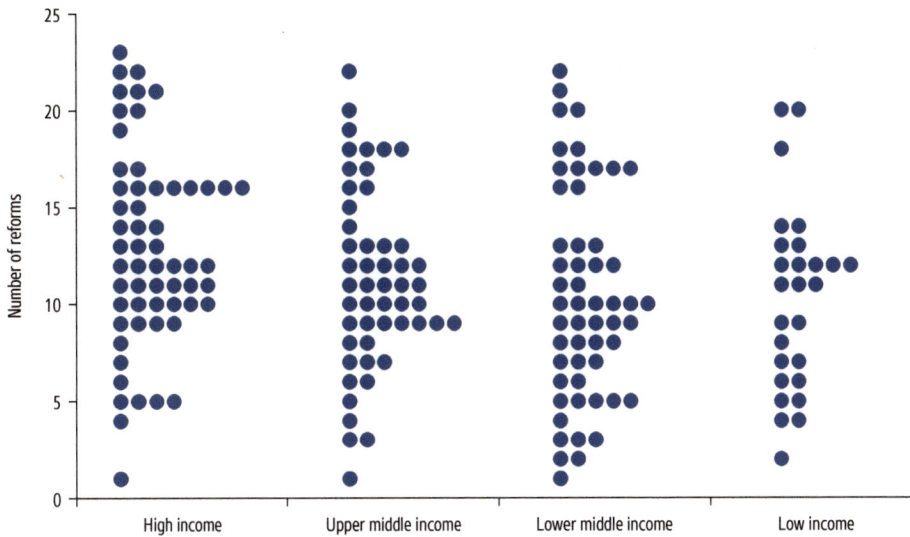

Source: Women, Business and the Law database.

Note: The figure shows for each economy, by income group, the number of reforms that removed legal gender barriers. A reform is counted if, within any of the 35 areas of measurement, an answer changes from "no" to "yes" because of the adoption of a new law or the amendment of an existing law. Each dot represents an economy. The income groups are constituted as follows: 58 high-income economies, 51 upper-middle-income economies, 54 lower-middle-income economies, and 27 low-income economies. All income groups are classified as of 2022, except for República Bolivariana de Venezuela, which is included in the upper-middle-income group, as last classified in 2021.

have implemented a total of 277 reforms, ranging from 2 (the Republic of Yemen) to 20 (the Democratic Republic of Congo and Togo) reforms. Reform efforts thus have not necessarily been restricted to higher-income economies.

Takeaway 3. Progress across the areas measured has also been uneven, with most reforms in Workplace and Parenthood.

Reform efforts across the 35 areas of measurement have differed substantially (figure 2.4). Across all indicators, most reforms have affected laws captured under Workplace and Parenthood. Under the Workplace indicator, many economies have been enacting laws that prohibit discrimination based on gender in employment (154 reforms) and address sexual harassment in employment (145 reforms).

As mentioned in chapter 1, Parenthood is still the indicator with the largest room for improvement overall, although economies have made some progress over time. For example, in 1989 Denmark was the first economy to reach a score of 100 on the Parenthood indicator. In the 1990s, 5 economies followed suit: Sweden (1991), Hungary (1992), Norway (1993), Belgium (1998), and Iceland (1998). By 2000, only 6 economies had reached a score of 100 on Parenthood; by the end of 2022, 35 economies had scored 100 on Parenthood. Overall, across regions OECD high-income economies reformed the most in the area of Parenthood across all eight areas of measurement (110 reforms).

FIGURE 2.4 | WORKPLACE HAS SEEN THE MOST AND MOBILITY THE LEAST NUMBER OF REFORMS ACROSS ALL EIGHT INDICATORS

Aggregate number of women's rights reforms, by indicator, 1970–2022

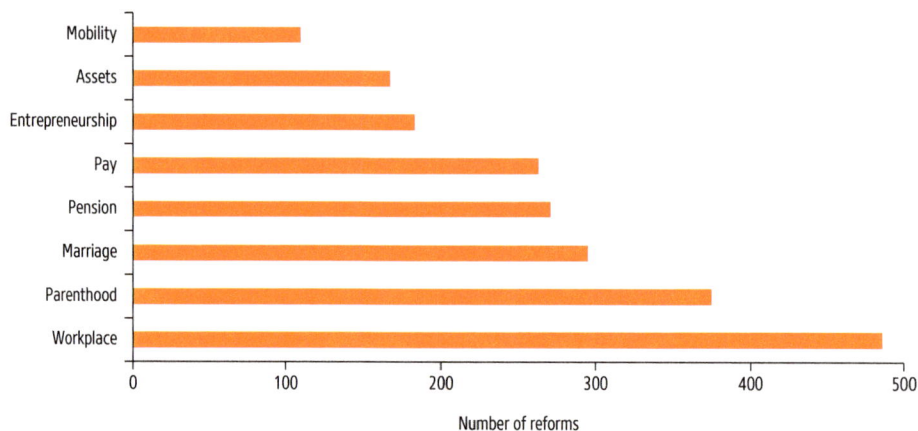

Source: Women, Business and the Law database.
Note: A reform is counted if, within any of the 35 areas of measurement, an answer changes from "no" to "yes" because of adoption of a new law or the amendment of an existing law.

By contrast, the fewest reforms have been issued on the Mobility indicator. This is because, in part, Mobility showed the highest level of equality at an aggregate level in 1970 and thus had the least room to improve among the eight areas of measurement. In particular, few reforms have been recorded on the question of whether women can travel outside the country (three reforms—one each in the Arab Republic of Egypt, Saudi Arabia, and the United Arab Emirates) and whether women can leave the marital home (six reforms—one each in Algeria, Italy, San Marino, Saudi Arabia, the Syrian Arab Republic, and the United Arab Emirates).

The gradual expansion of women's rights is not distributed equally across decades. Instead, reform efforts have unfolded in waves with a focus on specific areas. In the 1970s, economies largely removed gender barriers on mobility, allowing married women to choose where to live, and introduced legislation on the dismissal of pregnant workers. However, this process has not been consistent across regions. In the Middle East and North Africa, for example, reforms in the area of Mobility took off only in the 1990s. In the 1970s and 1980s, the region issued no reforms.

The 1980s, while continuing the reform efforts of the 1970s, was a decade of isolated breakthroughs. At the inception of the *Women, Business and the Law* panel data, Eritrea and Ethiopia were the only economies that already had legal provisions protecting women from sexual harassment. These provisions were enshrined in the penal code of 1957, which applied to both economies, as Eritrea and Ethiopia were one country until 1991. During the period covered by *Women, Business and the Law* panel data, the United States was the first economy to enact a reform protecting women from sexual harassment in employment, in 1981. The United States also enacted civil remedies for sexual harassment in employment. Soon after, Australia followed suit, enacting legislation to prohibit sexual harassment in all work-related activities.[13] Australia also prohibited gender discrimination in employment. In 1982,

Ireland was the first economy globally to introduce a specific law on domestic violence against women. Three economies followed Ireland's lead that decade: Hong Kong SAR, China; Singapore; and Sweden.

The 1990s set the stage for a steep increase in women's legal empowerment, with many economies making a foray into women's economic rights. For example, reform efforts were undertaken to mandate equal remuneration for work of equal value (19 reforms) and to grant women at least 14 weeks of paid maternity leave (10 reforms). Economies also issued 38 reforms introducing domestic violence legislation. These reform efforts have continued and, as a result, 162 economies have introduced domestic violence legislation, with the latest reforms passed by the Republic of Congo and Côte d'Ivoire in 2022.

The 2000s saw the most improvement across all areas measured, with a remarkable spike in reforms under the Workplace indicator. Although earlier reform efforts in this area concentrated on removing restrictions on getting a job, efforts in the 2000s continued introducing or reforming legislation on the prohibition of gender discrimination in employment as well as legislation on sexual harassment. These reform efforts, which have been most prevalent in Sub-Saharan Africa, may have been accelerated by the adoption of the Maputo Protocol by the African Union in 2003.

On a global level, as displayed in figure 2.5, moving toward gender equality in the law seems to follow a specific sequencing. Mobility and Assets—areas often regulated in economies' family law—were mostly reformed in the first two decades covered by *Women, Business and the Law*. About half of all reforms recorded in these two areas were

FIGURE 2.5 | WORKPLACE REFORMS SPIKED IN THE 1990s AND 2000s

Number of women's rights reforms, by decade

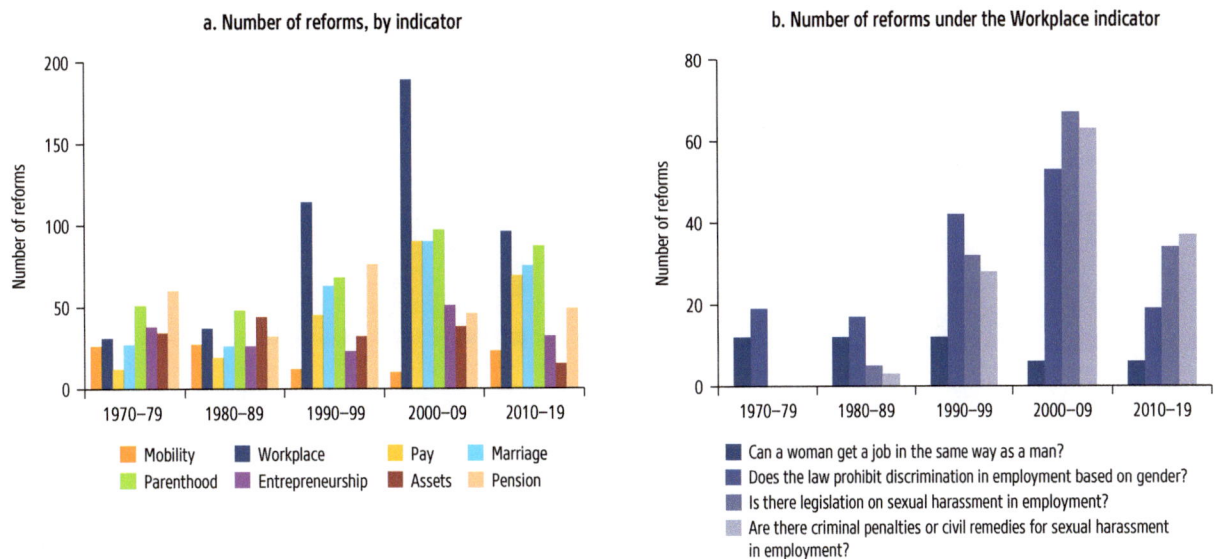

a. Number of reforms, by indicator

Legend: Mobility, Workplace, Pay, Marriage, Parenthood, Entrepreneurship, Assets, Pension

b. Number of reforms under the Workplace indicator

Legend:
- Can a woman get a job in the same way as a man?
- Does the law prohibit discrimination in employment based on gender?
- Is there legislation on sexual harassment in employment?
- Are there criminal penalties or civil remedies for sexual harassment in employment?

Source: Women, Business and the Law database.
Note: A reform is counted if, within any of the 35 areas of measurement, an answer changes from "no" to "yes" because of the adoption of a new law or the amendment of an existing law. To avoid suggesting a drop in reforms, the decade of the 2020s is omitted in this figure because only three years of data on reforms are available.

implemented before the end of the 1980s. In contrast, reforms in the areas of Pay and Workplace were very limited in the first two decades. The overarching majority of reforms in the area of Workplace (86 percent) were implemented in the 1990s and beyond. With regard to reforms in the area of Pay, about 71 percent of reforms have been implemented only since the turn of the century. Hence, more research is needed to shed light on whether reforming family laws is, in fact, a precondition for women's economic empowerment.

Despite these global trends, it is important to take country-specific or region-specific paths into account. At the inception of the *Women, Business and the Law* panel data, Czechia and the United Kingdom were the only two economies that already had legal provisions mandating equal remuneration for work of equal value. Somalia was then the first economy to introduce reforms mandating equal remuneration for work of equal value. Enacting a new labor code in 1972, Somalia prohibited gender discrimination in employment and the dismissal of pregnant workers and mandated equal remuneration for work of equal value. These reforms were the only ones that Somalia ever implemented, raising its *Women, Business and the Law* score from 32.5 to 49.9—a score that Somalia still holds today. Further, most other early reform efforts in the area of Pay were undertaken by OECD high-income economies (8 out of 12 in the 1970s). During the period covered by *Women, Business and the Law* panel data, France was the first European economy to introduce equal pay, in December 1972,[14] followed by Ireland, Luxembourg, and the Netherlands. One explanation for the region's relatively early adoption of reforms in the area of Pay could be the European Community's Equal Pay Directive,[15] which was adopted in February 1975.

Takeaway 4. Economies with historically larger legal gender gaps have been catching up, especially since 2000.

In 2022, despite global progress on reform, large gaps in legal equality remain between the most and the least equal economies. On the one hand, 14 economies have removed all legal inequalities in the areas covered by the *Women, Business and the Law* index. On the other hand, 16 economies still accord women fewer than half the rights of men. However, analysis of the log annualized growth rate in the *Women, Business and the Law* scores shows that faster progress is generally being made in economies that have had historically lower levels of gender equality. This catch-up effect, whereby economies that scored lower in 1970 experience a faster rate of reform growth over time, is illustrated in figure 2.6. Furthermore, because the *Women, Business and the Law* index is bounded between 0 and 100, economies with greater levels of legal equality have less room to improve than those with lower levels.

Figure 2.6 shows that the two economies with the fastest annual growth rates in the index (with growth rates, measured using log annualized rates, in the top percentile of the distribution) are São Tomé and Príncipe and the United Arab Emirates. These two economies, which have exhibited the highest log annualized growth rates in their score over the last 52 years, had among the lowest levels of legal gender equality in 1970 (scores of 17.5 and 18.75, respectively). While progress in the two economies has been similar, on average, there are large differences in the timing of reforms. In São Tomé and Príncipe, reform has been a gradual process since 1970, with periods when the pace of reform slowed and then, after a time, gathered pace again. In the United Arab Emirates, progress has been much more recent, with reforms taking off quickly since 2018.

FIGURE 2.6 | ECONOMIES WITH LESS GENDER-EQUAL LAWS IN 1970 ARE CATCHING UP

Women's rights reforms: The catch-up effect across economies

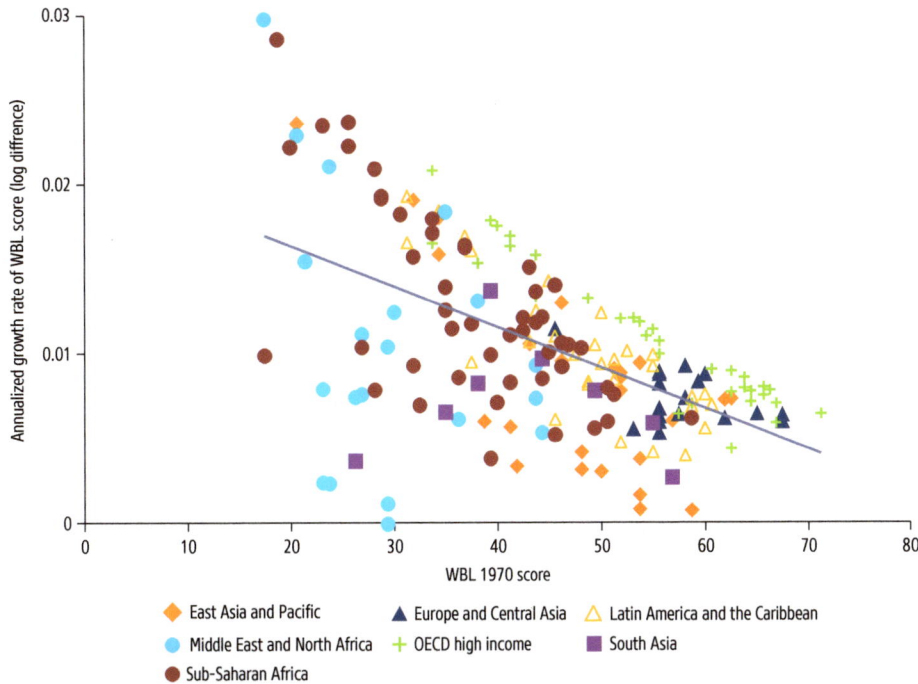

Source: Women, Business and Law database.
Note: The figure presents a statistical illustration of the catch-up effect by plotting each economy's log annualized average change in the *Women, Business and the Law* score, compared with its initial score in 1970. It shows that economies with lower scores in 1970, on average, had faster subsequent growth. All regions are classified as of 2022. OECD = Organisation for Economic Co-operation and Development.

Other economies that have experienced the fastest pace of reform—as measured by the log annualized growth rate of their *Women, Business and the Law* scores, which does not necessarily equate to the largest absolute change in the scores—are Bahrain, Botswana, the Democratic Republic of Congo, Indonesia, Saudi Arabia, South Africa, and Togo. In these seven economies, the average *Women, Business and the Law* score in 1970 was 22.8, which is far below the global average of 45.8 for the same year. In Botswana and the Democratic Republic of Congo, reform accelerated beginning in the 2000s, coinciding with the adoption of the Maputo Protocol and the golden decade for women's rights highlighted previously. In South Africa and Togo, reform had been taking place somewhat more consistently across the five decades, albeit with notable jumps when important legislative changes were made. In Bahrain and Saudi Arabia, as in the United Arab Emirates, reform has been a more recent phenomenon.

Indonesia is an interesting example of the path toward legal equality (figure 2.7). The first reform in Indonesia captured by the *Women, Business and the Law* panel data occurred in 1975, when articles of the Dutch civil code of 1847 were amended by the new Law No. 1 of 1974 on Marriage. Specifically, Article 66 of this law clarified

FIGURE 2.7 | THE CASE STUDY OF INDONESIA SHOWS THAT THE ROAD TO GENDER EQUALITY IS NOT ALWAYS A STRAIGHT LINE

Reforms in the Women, Business and the Law *index, Indonesia*

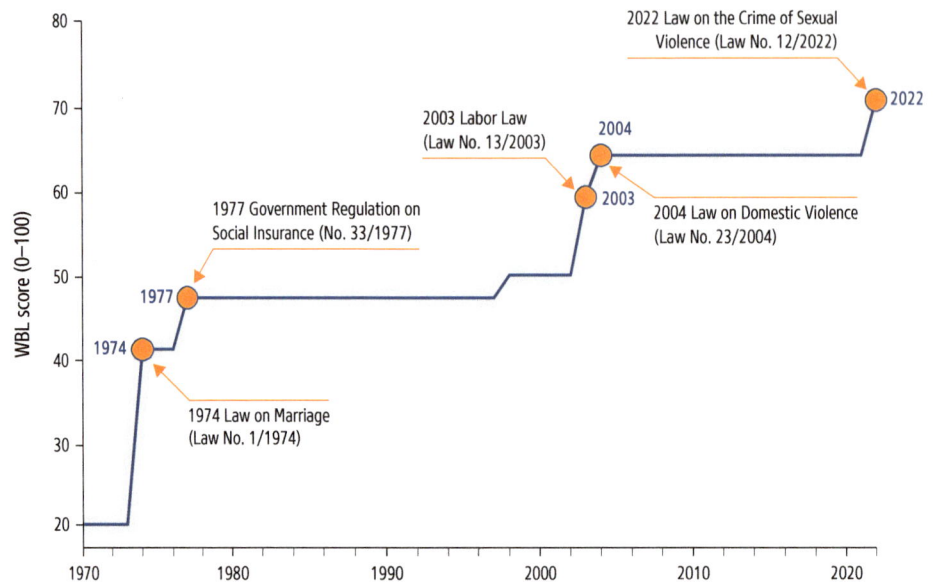

Source: Women, Business and the Law database.

that, with passage of the law, the articles in the civil code of 1847 pertaining to marriage were annulled, thus removing the historical restrictions on a woman's ability to act autonomously without the express permission of her husband. For example, as of 1975, married women in Indonesia could choose where to live, get a job, or sign a contract without facing restrictions that men did not face. By then, they also had greater rights related to ownership and management of assets. In total, seven data points across four indicators changed from "no" to "yes" because of this legal reform. Another important step toward ensuring a woman's economic rights occurred in 1977. Government Regulation No. 33/1977 on Social Insurance mandated equal retirement ages for men and women, contributing to women's economic security in later years.[16] This reform was followed by a long period from the mid-1970s to the mid-1990s during which Indonesia did not make strides toward legal equality. However, a period of notable progress followed: Indonesia's score jumped in 2004 with introduction of the 2003 Labor Law (Law No. 13/2003). This legislation prohibited discrimination based on gender in employment and removed historical restrictions on the tasks on, and industries in, which a woman could work. This reform was soon followed by passage of the Domestic Violence Law (Law No. 23/2004). Today, Indonesia continues to make important gains toward women's legal equality. As noted in chapter 1, in 2022 Indonesia enacted legislation protecting women from sexual harassment in employment and strengthening a woman's right to engage safely in paid work in the formal sector. Over the last five decades, Indonesia's legal landscape has progressed: in 1970, women had only 20 percent of the rights afforded to men; in 2022, they have just over 70 percent of these rights.

Despite Indonesia's positive trajectory, recent developments represent important setbacks on the path toward gender equality. Media have reported that, in October of 2022, a case of sexual assault occurred in the Ministry of Cooperatives and Small and Medium Enterprises and that attempts were made to settle the case by marrying the victim to the perpetrator (Bhwana 2022b). This took place in the same year that Indonesia enacted the 2022 Law on the Crime of Sexual Violence, a stark reminder of the gap that can exist between laws on the books and equality in practice. An additional setback occurred in December 2022, when Parliament passed a new criminal code containing provisions that, according to Human Rights Watch, are harmful to women, minorities, and free speech (Bhwana 2022a). In particular, a provision criminalizing consensual sex outside of marriage will disproportionately harm minorities, including women, who are more likely to be reported by their husbands for adultery (Human Rights Watch 2022). The new criminal code may also give formal legality to regulations imposed by local officials, including curfews for women and female genital mutilation (Human Rights Watch 2022). These provisions are outside the scope of what is currently measured by *Women, Business and the Law*, but they constitute clear obstacles to equality for women in Indonesia. Thus, the example of Indonesia illustrates how progress can be made in some areas of the law and subsequently undone in others.

While figure 2.6 illustrates that the pace of reform has been faster in historically less-equal economies, catch-up has not been a universal phenomenon. There are several examples of economies with scores that were well below the global average in 1970 and where the pace of reform, as measured by the log annualized growth in the scores, has been among the slowest. Most of these outliers are economies located in the Middle East and North Africa region. For example, Qatar's score is the same in 2022 as it was in 1970 (29.4), while the Islamic Republic of Iran's score increased by just under 2 points (from 29.4 to 31.3). In Sub-Saharan Africa, Sudan also has exhibited a low level of progress despite starting from a low base. In 1970, the *Women, Business and the Law* score in Sudan was 17.5 (the same as in the United Arab Emirates and the lowest score in the index); by 2022, the score had increased to only 29.4. This stark lack of progress points to the difficulty of reforming historically discriminatory laws in some economies and highlights that poorer performing economies will not necessarily catch up over time.

As discussed in the second takeaway, there have been differences among regions and income groups in how much progress has been made toward legal equality over the last five decades. These differences are confirmed by examining the average log annualized growth rate in the *Women, Business and the Law* score for each region since 1970. Overall, growth rates in the score, according to this metric, have been fastest in the Sub-Saharan Africa region, followed by OECD high-income economies. The average yearly growth rate in the score has been slowest in Europe and Central Asia, where legal equality was, on average, highest in 1970.

Not only are there differences between regions in how much progress has been made; the data also suggest that there are differences in the rate of catch-up within regions.[17] Table 2.1 presents a statistical illustration of the rate of catch-up between economies, within regions and income groups, as well as for different time periods. The negative coefficients suggest that, on average, catch-up is happening across the globe, with historically less-equal economies tending to reduce the gap in legal gender equality at a faster pace (column 1). Furthermore, the average pace of catch-up tends

TABLE 2.1	ECONOMIES THAT HAVE HISTORICALLY LAGGED BEHIND IN THE *WOMEN, BUSINESS AND THE LAW* INDEX HAVE BEEN CATCHING UP, 1970–2022			
	Regression results of the growth rate of WBL score on initial WBL value (dependent variable: growth rate of WBL score)			
Variable	**Overall (1)**	**Within region (2)**	**Within income groups (3)**	**Overall, pre- and post-2000 (4)**
Initial WBL score	−0.0100*** (−6.63)	−0.0146*** (−8.46)	−0.0112*** (−7.18)	
Initial WBL score for the period before 2000				−0.0086*** (−4.93)
Initial WBL score for the period after 2000				−0.0151*** (−8.77)
Fixed effects	None	Region	Income group	None

Source: Women, Business and the Law database.

Note: The table presents statistical illustrations of the degree to which economies have been catching up in the *Women, Business and the Law* index since 1970. Columns 1–3 present the coefficients from a regression of the annualized change in the log WBL score (1970–2022) on the log 1970 WBL score. The dependent variable is calculated by subtracting the 1970 log WBL score from the 2022 log WBL score and dividing by the total number of years (52). Column 4 presents the coefficients from a regression of the average annualized change in the log WBL score in two periods, pre-2000 (1970–99) and post-2000 (2000–22) on the initial log WBL score at the start of each period. The t values appear in parentheses. The "Initial WBL score for the period after 2000" coefficient is the summation of the pre-2000 coefficient and an interaction term. The corresponding value in parentheses is therefore an F statistic. The fixed-effect structure of the model is noted in the final row. All regressions include a constant term.

***$p < .01$.

to be faster among economies within the same region (column 2) and, to a lesser extent, within the same income group (column 3). The data also suggest that less gender-equal economies have been catching up approximately twice as fast since the turn of the century relative to the period before (column 4). To illustrate, based on the average speed of catch-up calculated across all economies and years (column 1), it will take another 64 years for an economy that is currently in the bottom 25th percentile on the *Women, Business and the Law* index (score of 68.12 in 2022) to close most legal gender gaps, denoted by a score of 90.

If instead we consider the rate of catch-up in the period after 2000 (as presented in column 4), an economy in the bottom 25th percentile will take another 42 years, on average, to reach a score of 90 on the *Women, Business and the Law* index. These illustrations of the possible length of time to approach legal equality are based on regression estimates from the panel data. They contrast with the estimate of 50 years presented previously, which was based on a projection forward of the pace of reform of just the most recent year. Different methodologies will lead to different conclusions, but, in all cases, the estimates suggest that women will have to wait several decades for all legal obstacles to equal economic opportunity to be removed.

Despite suggestions of catch-up across economies, as illustrated in figure 2.6 and table 2.1, differences in scores persist across economies and regions. There are notable disparities in the progress of regions toward reducing the variability of the *Women, Business and the Law* scores among their constituent economies. For example, there has been progress in how economies in the OECD high-income region have reduced the inequality in their scores. By contrast, progress over time has been much more uneven among economies in the Middle East and North Africa region, resulting in an overall increase in cross-country variability in legal equality since 1970. This increase may reflect the fact that, in the early years, reforms were being undertaken by relatively few economies within the region. For example, in the decade from 1970 to 1979, reforms were undertaken by only 6 of the 20 economies in the Middle East and North Africa region. In the 1980s, reforms were enacted in 5 economies. Since 2010, there has been progress in reducing the within-region variability in legal equality scores. This progress reflects the fact that the act of reforming laws has become more widespread. However, there remains substantial room for improvement.

Takeaway 5. The catch-up effect has been happening across all areas covered by Women, Business and the Law, but the pace of progress has been uneven.

All 35 areas of measurement have improved since the 1970s. However, the pace has differed across indicators (figure 2.8). Those indicators showing lower levels of legal equality in 1970 generally reformed at a faster pace. For example, progress toward legal equality as captured by Workplace, the indicator with the second-lowest average score in 1970, is striking. Altogether, the gender gap has been closing fastest in the laws affecting Workplace, followed by Parenthood. It has been closing slowest in laws related to Mobility and Assets.

The rate of catch-up within indicators reveals that, in all areas covered, economies that historically had lower scores have been making faster progress over time (table 2.2). The statistics presented in table 2.2 suggest that the rate of catch-up has been strong in the laws affecting women's decisions to enter and remain in the labor force (Workplace) as well as laws affecting their ability to start and run a business (Entrepreneurship). Considering changes in the Workplace indicator,

FIGURE 2.8 | HISTORICALLY MORE UNEQUAL AREAS HAVE REFORMED FASTER OVER TIME

Evolution of Women, Business and the Law indicator scores, 1970–2022

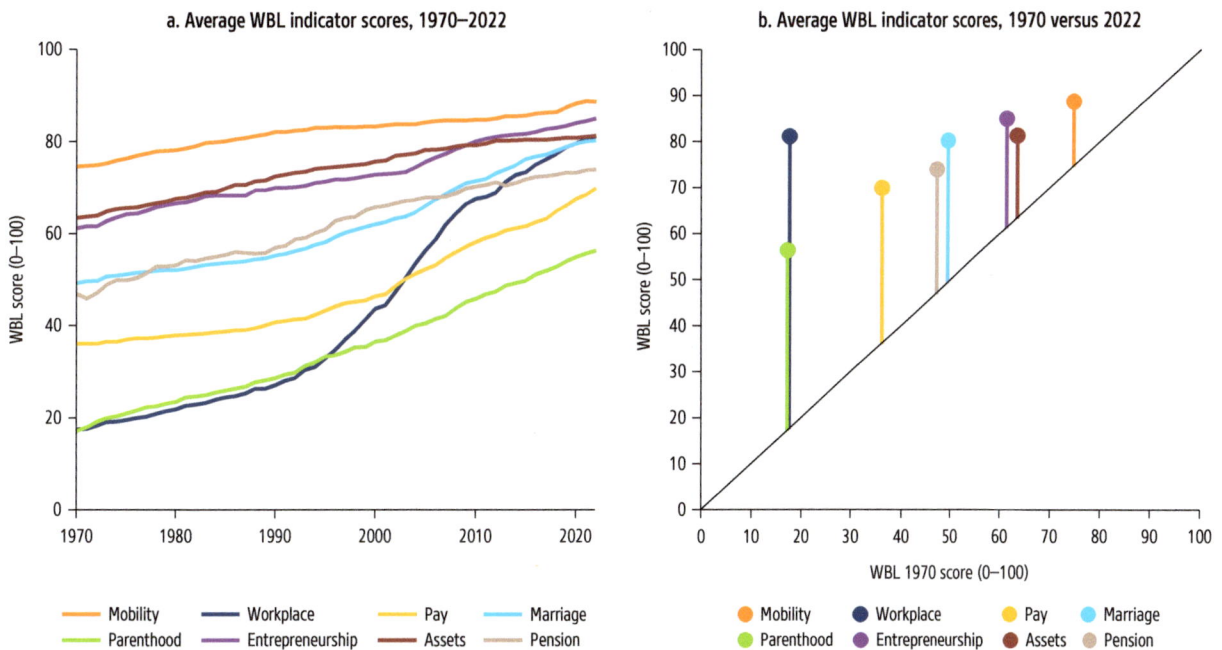

Source: Women, Business and the Law database.

TABLE 2.2	LOWER-SCORING ECONOMIES HAVE BEEN CATCHING UP WITHIN ALL EIGHT OF THE *WOMEN, BUSINESS AND THE LAW* INDICATORS, 1970–2022
	Regression results of the growth rate of WBL score on initial value, by indicator (dependent variable: growth rate of WBL indicator score)

Variable	Mobility	Workplace	Pay	Marriage	Parenthood	Entrepreneurship	Assets	Pension
Initial WBL indicator score	−0.0108*** (−19.18)	−0.0175*** (−25.80)	−0.0144*** (−19.12)	−0.0097*** (−13.75)	−0.0122*** (−13.39)	−0.0179*** (−41.79)	−0.0107*** (−14.27)	−0.0156*** (−16.60)

Source: Women, Business and the Law database.

Note: The table presents statistical illustrations of the degree to which economies have been catching up on the eight *Women, Business and the Law* indicators since 1970. Each column presents the coefficient from separate regressions of the annualized change in each of the eight WBL indicators' log score (1970–2022) on that indicator's log score in 1970. The dependent variable is calculated by subtracting the 1970 log WBL score from the 2022 log WBL score for each indicator and dividing by the total number of years (52). The *t* values appear in parentheses. Fixed effects are not included in these models. All regressions include a constant term.
***$p < .01$.

37 of the economies that scored 0 in the Workplace indicator in 1970 today receive a score of 100, indicating that all legal obstacles to women's work as measured by *Women, Business and the Law* have been removed. In the Entrepreneurship indicator, 15 economies increased their score from 0 in 1970 to 100 in 2022. In general, figure 2.8, panel a, shows flatter trend lines for those areas of the law that already scored above the index average in 1970; for example, in laws related to agency and freedom of movement (Mobility) and those related to property and inheritance rights (Assets). Only one economy has gone from 0 to 100 on either the Assets or the Mobility indicator (South Africa and the United Arab Emirates, respectively).

However, as with the degree of catch-up in the aggregate index, substantial variabilities are evident across economies and regions in each of the indicator scores. The evolution of this variability over time has followed a different pattern for each indicator as economies made progress in different areas of the law and at different points in time. While table 2.2 shows that the catch-up effect was happening within all indicators on aggregate, it says nothing about the possible sequencing of reforms. As discussed under the first main takeaway, at the global level, some indicators have seen an acceleration in progress before others.

When assessed at the regional level, there is some evidence that reforms happened under the Workplace indicator earlier than under the Pay indicator; however, the order in which *Women, Business and the Law* data points were reformed has varied across regions. For example, in South Asia, there was very little progress, on average, in either the Workplace or the Pay indicator up until the mid-1990s; at that point, reforms to laws captured under Workplace began to happen and took off in earnest from the middle to late 2000s. Reforms to the laws captured under Pay took place at a later point in time, but never accelerated as rapidly as reforms in the Workplace indicator.

There is also some evidence that, in the Middle East and North Africa region, reforms in the Pay indicator happened after reforms in the Workplace indicator. In 1970, the regional average score for the Pay indicator (20 points) was higher than the average regional score for the Workplace indicator (10 points). In the 2000s, the average pace of reform in the Workplace indicator accelerated quickly, which has kept up until very recent years. In laws captured by Pay, however, a similar level of acceleration is not seen until the late 2010s.

The pattern in the East Asia and Pacific region is different. Here, the average scores in Workplace and Pay in 1970 were 22 and 40 points, respectively. There was a rapid acceleration in the score under Workplace from the mid-1990s. By 2002, the average score in both indicators was the same (46 points); from this point onward, they moved in tandem. Indeed, today, the average score of the Workplace and Pay indicators are closest in the East Asia and Pacific region (at 71 and 72 points, respectively) than in any other region. Much more research, ideally at the economy level, is needed to understand the sequencing of reforms and its relevance to their successful implementation.

Evidence from the past can guide future decisions

Overcoming legal gender barriers benefits all of society—not just women. Increasing women's rights is an end in and of itself, but it also has sizable impacts on economies and societies at large. Advancing the rights of women has consistently been shown to bring a range of socioeconomic benefits (as discussed in the section on the benefits of legal gender reform). Therefore, economies should have a keen interest in empowering women because it opens a path to prosperity. Where women have more rights, freedoms, and opportunities, the whole economy experiences tangible, measurable gains. Furthermore, where women share equal rights with men in accessing economic opportunities, economies are stronger in the face of shocks arising from multiple, overlapping, and compounding crises such as the COVID-19 pandemic, the climate crisis, rising prices and food insecurity, and increased fragility and conflict. If everyone has an opportunity to participate, greater things can be achieved. And, as noted previously, economic and technological development can also be an important driver of gender equality, suggesting the possibility of a virtuous cycle of gender equality and economic development.

Progress is happening everywhere, but plenty of work remains on all fronts. Overcoming legal gender barriers is both a necessity and a reality that is happening in every economy, irrespective of its income level, culture, or region. As demonstrated, since 1970 all economies have enacted reforms to enhance women's economic empowerment, improving the global economy average score from 45.8 to 77.1 points. Some economies whose laws initially held more restrictions for women have shown impressive speed in overhauling legislation and expanding the legal rights of women, catching up with economies that historically have been more equal. But despite the progress achieved, much work still lies ahead. The size of the gap in women's rights determines the necessity of reform because the tangible impact for women may be largest in those economies that started off with the fewest rights. An additional 1,549 reforms are needed to reach legal gender equality everywhere, but only 34 were enacted last year. At this pace, it will take at least another 50 years to close the legal gender gap. Yet given the limited progress in some areas and specifically considering the low number of reforms in 2022, it may take much longer to close existing legal gender gaps across all areas. Even worse, some economies are reversing rights for which women have fiercely fought. Meanwhile, women worldwide have become important agents of change. They have been and still are taking to the streets to demand equal rights and opportunities, as protests in Argentina, Colombia, India, the Islamic Republic of Iran, Poland, the United States, and elsewhere vividly illustrate.

Better data to measure progress can be transformative. The *Women, Business and the Law* panel data presented in this report offer a framework for identifying gaps and entry points to assess economies' performance in closing legal gender gaps. Ground-breaking research has been using the *Women, Business and the Law* panel data set to uncover the motivations and benefits of reform (see box 2.1). Presenting these facts is a first step toward inspiring policy makers to remove existing discriminatory laws as well as promoting more research that uncovers the enabling factors needed to enhance women's economic inclusion. More, and better, data are needed to monitor progress toward gender equality and to understand the impacts of laws and policies on women, their families, and economies.

The *Women, Business and the Law* panel data offer a pathway to a substantial research agenda by exploring new topics that are fundamental to the effort to close persistent gender gaps in women's rights. These efforts include representative surveys at the individual level to measure the implications of laws on the ground, a study of laws at the subnational level to understand within-country variance, and coherent assessments of the drivers of reform to understand what underlying factors need to be in place for successful gender reform. Furthermore, *Women, Business and the Law* panel data allow for more research in areas that are notoriously data scarce: gender and climate and women's rights in fragile and conflict-affected regions.

More analysis is needed to understand the process of reform in order to accelerate gender equality everywhere. Women still face legal barriers in multiple domains, despite global progress. The data show that the catch-up of historically lower-performing economies is detectable and is happening more frequently within the same region or income group than the overall convergence globally, especially since 2000. More needs to be done to understand why. The pace of catch-up across economies could be correlated with several enabling factors, including political change, economic development, and growth in human capital as well as institutional reform more broadly. Understanding the relationship between the reform of gender discriminatory laws and other attributes is an important area for future research and is a priority area for identifying actionable policy recommendations.

The level of legal discrimination is particularly onerous in some highly populous countries and therefore restricts economic opportunities for a very large number of women. Removing structural barriers that constrain women's economic participation requires an enabling environment and collaborative engagements with multiple stakeholders. Furthermore, support from civil society actors and gender champions is essential to drive the reform agenda forward. That said, change will not come overnight. Reforming laws is an incremental process that requires the political will to find compromise and the ability to start conversations that would have been considered taboo in legislatures just a few years ago. Although great achievements have been made over the last five decades, more needs to be done worldwide to ensure that good intentions are accompanied by tangible results—that is, equal opportunity under the law for women. Women cannot afford to wait another 50 years or more to reach equality. Neither can the global economy.

Notes

1. Panel data are available at https://wbl.worldbank.org/en/wbl-data and on the World Bank's Gender Data Portal at https://genderdata.worldbank.org/.
2. A previous version of the panel data set has already been publicized on the *Women, Business and the Law* website. Since then, the data have been expanded, updated, and revised. In order to provide a comparable time-series data set, any data revisions are back-calculated to 1970.

3. A reform is counted if an economy reforms a law that affects any of the 35 areas of measurement resulting in a change of answers from "no" to "yes." As such, a reform is counted each time a legal restriction formerly placed on women is removed in the law. For example, Uganda's 2022 Succession (Amendment) Act resulted in a count of three reforms because answers in the following areas changed from "no" to "yes": Do sons and daughters have equal rights to inherit assets from their parents? Do female and male surviving spouses have equal rights to inherit assets? Can a woman choose where to live in the same way as a man? Reversal of rights on progress that has already been made in an economy toward women's full economic empowerment (a change from "yes" to "no") along with legal changes that do not affect the 35 areas of measurement (legal changes that still result in a "yes" answer for the 35 areas) are not counted as a reform.

4. Labour Code of 1972, Art. 91.

5. Ley de Contrato de Trabajo de 1974, Art. 193.

6. Employment Insurance Act, Secs. 12(4.01) and 23.

7. These economies are Bahrain, Botswana, the Democratic Republic of Congo, Indonesia, Jordan, Kuwait, the Republic of Yemen, São Tomé and Príncipe, Saudi Arabia, Sudan, the United Arab Emirates, and the West Bank and Gaza.

8. On April 14, 2008, the Republic of Yemen enacted Law No. 15 of 2008 amending the labor code (Act No. 5 of 1995).

9. African Union, Status of Implementation of the Protocol to the African Charter on Human and People's Rights on the Rights of Women in Africa, https://www.peaceau.org/uploads/special-rapporteur-on-rights-of-women-in-africa-presentation-for-csw-implementation.pdf.

10. By contrast, in 2019 Nepal introduced a restriction on women's rights, making it more difficult for women to choose where to live.

11. Act No. XXI of 1993 amending Article 1322 (1) of the civil code.

12. República Bolivariana de Venezuela is included in the upper-middle-income group, as last classified in 2021.

13. Sex Discrimination Act 1984, Sec. 22B.

14. France enacted Loi No. 72-1143 du 22 décembre 1972 relative à l'égalité de rémunération entre les hommes et les femmes, outlining in Article 1 that an employer is obliged to ensure, for the same work or for work of equal value, equal remuneration for men and women.

15. Council Directive 75/117/EEC of 10 February 1975 on the approximation of the laws of the member states relating to the application of the principle of equal pay for men and women.

16. This regulation was also repealed in 1993 by Government Regulation No. 14/1993 on the Provision of Social Insurance Programs for Workers, but this change does not result in any changes in the *Women, Business and the Law* score.

17. The rate of catch-up is proportional to the absolute value of the estimated regression coefficient.

References

Affoum, Nelsy Reyhanne Marikel, and Marie Jeanne Charlotte Dry. 2022. "Reforming Discriminatory Laws to Empower Women in Togo." Global Indicators Brief 12, World Bank, Washington, DC.

Agarwal, Bina. 2003. "Gender and Land Rights Revisited: Exploring New Prospects via the State, Family, and Market." *Journal of Agrarian Change* 3 (1–2): 184–224.

Alemayehu, Maereg Tewoldebirhan, Viktoria Khaitina, Elshaday Kifle Woldeyesus, Olena Mykhalchenko, and Katrin Schulz. Forthcoming. "The Road to Reforming Ethiopia's Maternity and Paternity Leave Policies." Global Indicators Brief, World Bank, Washington, DC.

Amin, Mohammad, and Asif M. Islam. 2015. "Does Mandating Non-discrimination in Hiring Practices Influence Women's Employment? Evidence Using Firm-Level Data." *Feminist Economics* 21 (4): 28–60. doi:10.1080/13545701.2014.1000354.

Amin, Mohammad, and Asif M. Islam. 2022. "The Impact of Paid Maternity Leave on Women's Employment." Policy Research Working Paper 10188, World Bank, Washington, DC.

Anderson, Siwan. 2018. "Legal Origins and Female HIV." *American Economic Review* 108 (6): 1407–39. doi.org/10.1257/aer.20151047.

Arekapudi, Nisha, and Nátalia Silva Martins Mazoni. 2022. "Challenging Entrenched Marital Power in South Africa." Global Indicators Brief 6, World Bank, Washington, DC.

Asiedu, Elizabeth, Claire Branstette, Neepa Gaekwad-Babulal, and Nanivazo Malokele. 2018. "The Effect of Women's Representation in Parliament and the Passing of Gender Sensitive Policies." Paper presented at Allied Social Science Association (ASSA) Annual Meeting, Philadelphia, January 5–7, 2018.

Bertrand, Jérémie, and Caroline Perrin. 2022. "Girls Just Wanna Have Funds? The Effect of Women-Friendly Legislation on Female-Led Firms' Access to Credit." *International Review of Law and Economics* 72 (December): 106101. doi.org/10.1016/j.irle.2022.106101.

Bhwana, Petir Garda. 2022a. "Human Rights Watch: New Criminal Code Harmful to Women, Minorities, Free Speech." *Tempo.co,* December 8, 2022. https://en.tempo.co/read/1665967/human-rights -watch-new-criminal-code-harmful-to-women-minorities-free-speech.

Bhwana, Petir Garda. 2022b. "Sexual Assault Case Emerges from State Ministry." *Tempo.co,* October 26, 2022. https://en.tempo.co/read/1649485/sexual-assault-case-emerges-from-state-ministry.

Branisa, Boris, Stephan Klasen, and Maria Ziegler. 2013. "Gender Inequality in Social Institutions and Gendered Development Outcomes." *World Development* 45 (May): 252–68.

Braunmiller, Julia Constanze, and Marie Dry. 2022. "Reforms to Enhance Gender Equality in the Democratic Republic of Congo: From Advocacy to Implementation." Global Indicators Brief 4, World Bank, Washington, DC.

Braunmiller, Julia Constanze, Isabel Santagostino Recavarren, Aparna Mittal, and Tanvi Khatri. Forthcoming. "How Did India Successfully Reform Women's Rights? Answers from the Movements on Equal Inheritance Rights and Protection from Violence." Global Indicators Brief, World Bank, Washington, DC.

Christopherson, Katharine, Audrey Yiadom, Juliet Johnson, Francisca Fernando, Hanan Yazid, and Clara Thiemann. 2022. "Tackling Legal Impediments to Women's Economic Empowerment." IMF Working Paper WP/22/37, International Monetary Fund, Washington, DC.

Deininger, Klaus, Aparajita Goyal, and Hari Nagarajan. 2013. "Women's Inheritance Rights and Intergenerational Transmission of Resources in India." *Journal of Human Resources* 48 (1): 114–41. doi:10.3368/jhr.48.1.114.

Deininger, Klaus, Songqing Jin, Hari K. Nagarajan, and Fang Xia. 2019. "Inheritance Law Reform, Empowerment, and Human Capital Accumulation: Second-Generation Effects from India." *Journal of Development Studies* 55 (12): 2549–71.

Deininger, Klaus, Fang Xia, Talip Kilic, and Heather Moyland. 2021. "Investment Impacts of Gendered Land Rights in Customary Tenure Systems: Substantive and Methodological Insights from Malawi." *World Development* 147 (November): 105654. doi.org/10.1016/j.worlddev.2021.105654.

Demirgüç-Kunt, Aslı, Leora Klapper, and Dorothe Singer. 2013. "Financial Inclusion and Legal Discrimination against Women: Evidence from Developing Countries." Policy Research Working Paper 6416, World Bank, Washington, DC.

Doepke, Matthias, and Michèle Tertilt. 2009. "Women's Liberation: What's in It for Men?" *Quarterly Journal of Economics* 124 (4): 1541–91. doi.org/10.1162/qjec.2009.124.4.1541.

Doepke, Matthias, Michèle Tertilt, and Alessandra Voena. 2012. "The Economics and Politics of Women's Rights." *Annual Review of Economics* 4 (1): 339–72.

Duflo, Esther. 2012. "Women Empowerment and Economic Development." *Journal of Economic Literature* 50 (4): 1051–79. doi:10.1257/jel.50.4.1051.

Eastin, Joshua, and Aseem Prakash. 2013. "Economic Development and Gender Equality: Is There a Gender Kuznets Curve?" *World Politics* 65 (1): 156–86.

Geddes, Rick, and Dean Lueck. 2002. "The Gains from Self-Ownership and the Expansion of Women's Rights." *American Economic Review* 92 (4): 1079–92.

Githae, Catherine Nyaguthii, Emilia Galiano, Fredrick Josphat Kibuti Nyagah, and Isabel Micaela Santagostino Recavarren. 2022. "Key Ingredients to Women's Legal Rights in Kenya." Global Indicators Brief 5, World Bank, Washington, DC.

Goldman, Wendy Z. 1993. *Women, the State, and Revolution: Soviet Family Policy and Social Life, 1917–1936.* Cambridge, UK: Cambridge University Press.

Gonzales, Christian, Sonali Jain-Chandra, Kalpana Kochhar, and Monique Newiak. 2015. "Fair Play: More Equal Laws Boost Female Labor Force Participation." IMF Staff Discussion Note SDN/15/02, International Monetary Fund, Washington, DC.

Hallward-Driemeier, Mary, Tazeen Hasan, and Anca B. Rusu. 2013. "Women's Legal Rights over 50 Years: What Is the Impact of Reform?" Policy Research Working Paper 6617, World Bank, Washington, DC.

Harari, Mariaflavia. 2019. "Women's Inheritance Rights and Bargaining Power: Evidence from Kenya." *Economic Development and Cultural Change* 68 (1): 189–238. doi.org/10.1086/700630.

Hazan, Moshe, David Weiss, and Hosny Zoabi. 2021. "Women's Liberation, Household Revolution." CEPR Discussion Paper 16838, Center for Economic and Policy Research, Washington, DC.

Htun, Mala, Francesca Jensenius, and Jami Nelson-Nuñez. 2019. "Gender-Discriminatory Laws and Women's Economic Agency." *Social Politics: International Studies in Gender, State, and Society* 26 (2): 193–222. doi:10.1093/sp/jxy042.

Htun, Mala, and S. Laurel Weldon. 2011. "State Power, Religion, and Women's Rights: A Comparative Analysis of Family Law." *Indiana Journal of Global Legal Studies* 18 (1): 145–65.

Htun, Mala, and S. Laurel Weldon. 2015. "Religious Power, the State, Women's Rights, and Family Law." *Politics & Gender* 11 (3): 451–77.

Human Rights Watch. 2022. "Indonesia: New Criminal Code Disastrous for Rights." *Human Rights Watch,* December 8, 2022. https://www.hrw.org/news/2022/12/08/indonesia -new-criminal-code-disastrous-rights.

Hyland, Marie, Simeon Djankov, and Pinelopi Koujianou Goldberg. 2020. "Gendered Laws and Women in the Workforce." *American Economic Review: Insights* 2 (4): 475–90.

Hyland, Marie, and Asif Islam. 2021. "Gendered Laws, Informal Origins, and Subsequent Performance." Policy Research Working Paper 9766, World Bank, Washington, DC.

Hyland, Marie, and Liang Shen. 2022. "The Evolution of Maternity and Paternity Leave Policies over Five Decades: A Global Analysis." Policy Research Working Paper 10215, World Bank, Washington, DC.

Islam, Asif, Silvia Muzi, and Mohammad Amin. 2019. "Unequal Laws and the Disempowerment of Women in the Labour Market: Evidence from Firm-Level Data." *Journal of Development Studies* 55 (5): 822–44.

Jung, Hoyong. 2022. "Female Leaders and Gendered Laws: A Long-Term Global Perspective." *International Political Science Review* 1–19. doi.org/10.1177/01925121221095439.

Kang, Alice J. 2015. *Bargaining for Women's Rights: Activism in an Aspiring Muslim Democracy.* Minneapolis: University of Minnesota Press.

Lapidus, Gail Warshofsky. 1978. *Women in Soviet Society: Equality, Development and Social Change.* Berkeley: University of California Press.

Lizzeri, Alessandro, and Nicola Persico. 2004. "Why Did the Elites Extend the Suffrage? Democracy and the Scope of Government, with an Application to Britain's 'Age of Reform.'" *Quarterly Journal of Economics* 119 (2): 707–65. doi.org/10.1162/0033553041382175.

Lo Bue, Maria C., Tu Thi Ngoc Le, Manuel Santos Silva, and Kunal Sen. 2022. "Gender and Vulnerable Employment in the Developing World: Evidence from Global Microdata." *World Development* 159 (November): 106010. doi.org/10.1016/j.worlddev.2022.106010.

Macaulay, Fiona. 2002. "Taking the Law into Their Own Hands: Women, Legal Reform, and Legal Literacy in Brazil." In *Gender and the Politics of Rights and Democracy in Latin America*, edited by Nikke Craske and Maxine Molyneux, 79–101. Women's Studies at York Series. London: Palgrave Macmillan.

Mazoni Silva Martins, Nátalia, and Claudia Lenny Corminales. 2022. "Legal Reforms to Protect Women at Home and at Work in São Tomé and Príncipe." Global Indicators Brief 13, World Bank, Washington, DC.

Moustafa, Tamir. 2013. "Islamic Law, Women's Rights, and Popular Legal Consciousness in Malaysia." *Law & Social Inquiry* 38 (1): 168–88.

Perrin, Caroline, and Marie Hyland. 2023. "Gendered Laws and Women's Financial Inclusion." World Bank, Washington, DC.

Roy, Sanchari. 2019. "Discriminatory Laws against Women: A Survey of the Literature." Policy Research Working Paper 8719, World Bank, Washington, DC.

Sever, Can. 2022a. "Gendered Laws and Labour Force Participation." *Applied Economics Letters*. doi/abs/10.1 080/13504851.2022.2103078.

Sever, Can. 2022b. "Legal Gender Equality as a Catalyst for Convergence." IMF Working Paper WP/22/155, International Monetary Fund, Washington, DC.

Shachar, Ayelet. 2001. *Multicultural Jurisdictions: Cultural Differences and Women's Rights.* New York: Cambridge University Press.

Tertilt, Michèle, Matthias Doepke, Anne Hannusch, and Laura Montenburck. 2022. "The Economics of Women's Rights." NBER Working Paper 30617, National Bureau of Economic Research, Cambridge, MA.

Weldon, S. Laurel. 2002. *Protest, Policy, and the Problem of Violence against Women: A Cross-National Comparison.* Pittsburgh: University of Pittsburgh Press.

Wolchik, Sharon. 1995. "Gender Issues during Transition." In *East-Central European Economies in Transition*, edited by John Pearce Hardt and Richard F. Kaufman, 147–70. Armonk, NY: M. E. Sharpe.

World Bank. 2022. *United Arab Emirates (UAE): Legal Reforms to Strengthen Women's Economic Inclusion— Case Study.* Equitable Growth, Finance and Institutions Notes. Washington, DC: World Bank Group.

| # Data Notes

Women, Business and the Law measures laws and regulations affecting women's economic inclusion in 190 economies. Although progress has been made over the last 53 years, the data confirm that more work is needed to ensure that women have equality of opportunity when entering the workforce and starting their own businesses. To highlight these opportunities for change, *Women, Business and the Law 2023* presents an index structured around the stages of a woman's working life (figure A.1).

This framework helps to align areas of the law with the economic decisions that women make as they experience various milestones. The indicators not only represent women's interactions with the law as they begin, progress through, and end their careers, but also are easily replicable measures of the legal environment that women must navigate as entrepreneurs and employees. This edition of *Women, Business and the Law* presents an update of the index, taking into account the laws and regulations reformed between October 2, 2021, and October 1, 2022.

FIGURE A.1 | THE EIGHT *WOMEN, BUSINESS AND THE LAW* INDICATORS

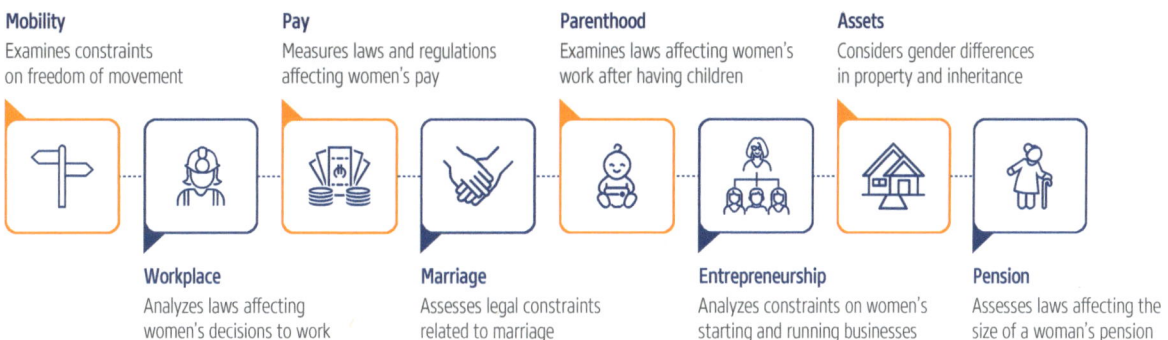

Mobility
Examines constraints on freedom of movement

Pay
Measures laws and regulations affecting women's pay

Parenthood
Examines laws affecting women's work after having children

Assets
Considers gender differences in property and inheritance

Workplace
Analyzes laws affecting women's decisions to work

Marriage
Assesses legal constraints related to marriage

Entrepreneurship
Analyzes constraints on women's starting and running businesses

Pension
Assesses laws affecting the size of a woman's pension

Source: Women, Business and the Law team.

Methodology

Women, Business and the Law is based on an analysis of the domestic laws and regulations that affect women's economic opportunities. The indicators were selected on the basis of their association with measures of women's economic empowerment and through research and consultation with experts. They are also in line with the international legal frameworks set out in the Convention on the Elimination of All Forms of Discrimination against Women (CEDAW); the Committee on the Elimination of Discrimination against Women General Recommendations (CEDAW GR); the United Nations (UN) Declaration on the Elimination of Violence against Women (DEVAW); and the International Labour Organization (ILO) Equal Remuneration Convention, 1951 (No. 100), the Discrimination (Employment and Occupation) Convention, 1958 (No. 111), the Maternity Protection Convention, 2000 (No. 183), and the Violence and Harassment Convention, 2019 (No. 190).

TABLE A.1	*WOMEN, BUSINESS AND THE LAW* INDICATORS
Indicator	**Questions**
Mobility	1. Can a woman choose where to live in the same way as a man?
	2. Can a woman travel outside her home in the same way as a man?
	3. Can a woman apply for a passport in the same way as a man?
	4. Can a woman travel outside the country in the same way as a man?
Workplace	1. Can a woman get a job in the same way as a man?
	2. Does the law prohibit discrimination in employment based on gender?
	3. Is there legislation on sexual harassment in employment?
	4. Are there criminal penalties or civil remedies for sexual harassment in employment?
Pay	1. Does the law mandate equal remuneration for work of equal value?
	2. Can a woman work at night in the same way as a man?
	3. Can a woman work in a job deemed dangerous in the same way as a man?
	4. Can a woman work in an industrial job in the same way as a man?
Marriage	1. Is the law free of legal provisions that require a married woman to obey her husband?
	2. Can a woman be head of household in the same way as a man?
	3. Is there legislation specifically addressing domestic violence?
	4. Can a woman obtain a judgment of divorce in the same way as a man?
	5. Does a woman have the same rights to remarry as a man?
Parenthood	1. Is paid leave of at least 14 weeks available to mothers?
	2. Does the government administer 100% of maternity leave benefits?
	3. Is paid leave available to fathers?
	4. Is there paid parental leave?
	5. Is dismissal of pregnant workers prohibited?
Entrepreneurship	1. Does the law prohibit discrimination in access to credit based on gender?
	2. Can a woman sign a contract in the same way as a man?
	3. Can a woman register a business in the same way as a man?
	4. Can a woman open a bank account in the same way as a man?
Assets	1. Do men and women have equal ownership rights to immovable property?
	2. Do sons and daughters have equal rights to inherit assets from their parents?
	3. Do male and female surviving spouses have equal rights to inherit assets?
	4. Does the law grant spouses equal administrative authority over assets during marriage?
	5. Does the law provide for the valuation of nonmonetary contributions?
Pension	1. Is the age at which men and women can retire with full pension benefits the same?
	2. Is the age at which men and women can retire with partial pension benefits the same?
	3. Is the mandatory retirement age for men and women the same?
	4. Are periods of absence due to childcare accounted for in pension benefits?

Source: Women, Business and the Law database.
Note: The index scores 35 data points across eight indicators composed of four or five binary questions, with each indicator representing a different phase of a woman's life. Indicator-level scores are obtained by calculating the unweighted average of responses to the questions within that indicator and scaling the result to 100. For each question, Y = 1 and N = 0. Overall scores are then calculated by taking the average of each indicator, with 100 representing the highest possible score.

FIGURE A.2 | SAMPLE SCORING ON THE *WOMEN, BUSINESS AND THE LAW* INDEX: ECUADOR

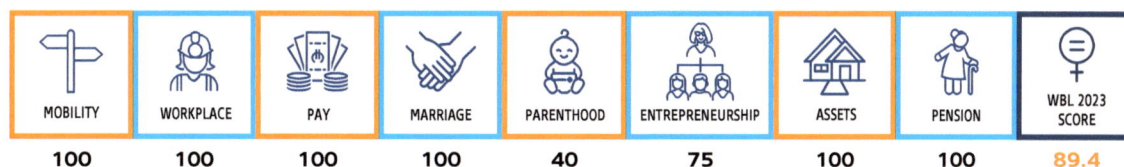

MOBILITY	WORKPLACE	PAY	MARRIAGE	PARENTHOOD	ENTREPRENEURSHIP	ASSETS	PENSION	WBL 2023 SCORE
100	100	100	100	40	75	100	100	89.4

Source: *Women, Business and the Law* database.

The data set and analysis can be used to support research and policy discussions on the ways in which the legal environment influences women's economic activity. Thirty-five data points are scored across eight indicators composed of four or five binary questions, with each indicator representing a different phase of a woman's life (table A.1). Indicator-level scores are obtained by calculating the unweighted average of responses to the questions within that indicator and scaling the result to 100. Overall scores are then calculated by taking the average of each indicator, with 100 representing the highest possible score.

Examining the data for one economy illustrates how scoring works in the index. Ecuador, for example, receives a score of 100 for Mobility, Workplace, Pay, Marriage, Assets, and Pension, which indicates that no legal constraints are found in the areas measured under these indicators (figure A.2).

Under Parenthood, however, the lack of at least 14 weeks of paid maternity leave, government-administered maternity leave benefits, or paid parental leave results in a score of 40. The score for Entrepreneurship is 75 because the law does not prohibit gender-based discrimination in access to credit.

Based on this information, the overall score for Ecuador is calculated as the unweighted average of all eight indicator scores on a scale of 0–100, with 100 representing the best score overall. Ecuador thus scores 89.4 on the *Women, Business and the Law* index.

Strengths and limitations of the methodology

To construct the index, *Women, Business and the Law* relies on feedback from more than 2,400 respondents with expertise in family, labor, and criminal law, including lawyers, judges, academics, and members of civil society organizations working locally on gender issues. Besides filling out written questionnaires, respondents provide references to relevant legislation. The *Women, Business and the Law* team then collects the texts of these laws and regulations and verifies questionnaire responses for accuracy. Responses are validated against codified sources of national law, including constitutions, codes, laws, statutes, rules, regulations, and procedures in areas such as labor, social security, civil procedure, violence against women, marriage and family, inheritance, nationality, and land. The data reflect legislation in force as of October 1, 2022.

This unique approach has both strengths and limitations (table A.2). Because the indicators are binary, they may not reflect the nuances or details of some of the policies measured.

TABLE A.2	METHODOLOGICAL STRENGTHS AND LIMITATIONS OF THE *WOMEN, BUSINESS AND THE LAW* INDEX	
Feature	**Strength**	**Limitation**
Use of standardized assumptions	Data are comparable across economies, and methodology is transparent.	The scope of data is smaller; only regulatory reforms in the areas measured can be tracked systematically.
Coverage of largest business city only	Data collection is manageable, and data are comparable.	In federal economies, data may be less representative where laws differ across locations.
Focus on the most populous group	Data are comparable across economies where parallel legal systems prescribe different rights for different groups of women.	Restrictions that apply to minority populations may not be captured.
Emphasis on the formal sector	Attention remains centered on the formal economy, where regulations are most relevant.	The reality faced by women in the informal sector, which may be a significant population in some economies, is not fully reflected.
Measure of codified laws only	Indicators are actionable because the law is what policy makers can change.	Where systematic implementation of legislation is lacking, regulatory changes alone will not achieve the desired results; social and cultural norms are not considered.

Source: Women, Business and the Law team.

Indicators are also based on standardized assumptions to ensure comparability across economies. For example, an assumption used for questions on maternity leave is that the woman in question has one child. Although maternity leave benefits often differ for multiple births, only data for individual births are captured. Another assumption is that the woman in question is located in the largest business city of the economy. In federal economies, laws affecting women can vary by state or province. Even in nonfederal economies, women in rural areas and small towns could face more restrictive local legislation. *Women, Business and the Law* does not capture such restrictions unless they are also found in the main business city. Finally, where personal law prescribes different rights and obligations for different groups of women, the data focus on the most populous group. Thus, the study may not capture restrictions applying only to minority populations.

Although it ensures comparability of the data, the use of standardized assumptions has a limited ability to reflect the full diversity of women's experiences. *Women, Business and the Law* recognizes that the laws it measures do not apply to all women in the same way. Women face intersectional forms of discrimination based not only on gender and sex but also on sexuality, race, gender identity, religion, family status, ethnicity, nationality, disability, and many other grounds. *Women, Business and the Law* therefore encourages readers to interpret the data in conjunction with other available research.

Women, Business and the Law focuses on the ways in which the official legal and regulatory environment regulates how women can work or operate their own businesses. While the attention is centered on the formal economy—that is, in jobs that provide social protection and other entitlements through formal arrangements—half of the indicators have direct relevance for women working in the informal sector. The data captured by *Women, Business and the Law* can be relevant for women regardless of their official employment status. For example, laws affecting women's agency and mobility, ability to own or inherit property, or protections against domestic violence apply to women in both formal and informal employment. Additionally, legal protections affecting the workplace provide a foundation for economic inclusion and offer incentives for women to enter and remain in the labor force. Laws affecting women's mobility and agency within households directly affect their ability to start and operate registered businesses. Although many women in developing economies work informally, this project aims to define some of the features of the legal framework that enable women to transition from the informal to the formal economy.

This project also recognizes the often large gaps between laws on the books and actual practice. One reason for these gaps may be poor implementation of legislation stemming from weak enforcement, poor design, or low institutional capacity. Nonetheless, identifying legal differences is one step toward better understanding where women's economic rights may be restricted in practice.

Women, Business and the Law acknowledges that equal opportunities for women in business and the workplace depend on an interplay of economic, social, and cultural factors. For example, unless women are able to get an education or build their skills, equalizing laws affecting entrepreneurship and employment could mean little. Other factors, such as infrastructure, also may affect the ability and desire of women to work. In addition, social and cultural norms may prevent women from running a business or working outside the home. Within this overall picture, *Women, Business and the Law* recognizes the limitations of its assumptions and its focus on statutory law. Even though such assumptions may come at the expense of specificity, they also ensure data comparability across economies.

Indicators and questions

This section looks more closely at the 35 scored binary questions, grouped by indicator (box A.1). Answers to the questions are based on codified law only. Customary law is not considered unless it has been codified. Where the answer differs according to the legal system (for example, in mixed legal systems where different laws govern different groups of people within an economy), the answer used is the one that applies to the majority of the population. Supranational law, such as that enacted by the Organization for the Harmonization of Business Law in Africa (OHADA), is not considered where domestic law contravenes supranational rules and limits the legal capacity of women. This section details by indicator how answers are standardized and made comparable across all economies.

BOX A.1 ASSUMPTIONS USED TO ENSURE COMPARABILITY

The woman in question

- Resides in the economy's main business city;
- Has reached the legal age of majority and is capable of making decisions as an adult, is in good health, and has no criminal record;
- Is a lawful citizen of the economy being examined;
- Is a cashier in the food retail sector in a supermarket or grocery store that has 60 employees;
- Is a cisgender, heterosexual woman in a monogamous first marriage registered with the appropriate authorities (de facto marriages and customary unions are not measured);
- Is of the same religion as her husband;

(Box continues next page)

BOX A.1 ASSUMPTIONS USED TO ENSURE COMPARABILITY *(continued)*

- Is in a marriage under the rules of the default marital property regime or the most common regime for that jurisdiction, which will not change during the course of the marriage; and
- Is not a member of a union unless membership is mandatory. Membership is considered mandatory when collective bargaining agreements cover more than 50 percent of the workforce in the food retail sector and when they apply to individuals who were not party to the original collective bargaining agreement.

For the questions on maternity, paternity, and parental leave, it is assumed that

- The woman gave birth to her first child without complications on October 1, 2022, and her child is in good health. Answers will therefore correspond to legislation in force as of October 1, 2022, even if the law provides for changes over time.
- Both parents have been working long enough to accrue any maternity, paternity, and parental benefits.
- If maternity benefit systems are not mandatory or were not operational as of October 1, 2022, they are not measured.

For the questions on inheritance rights, it is assumed that

- The deceased has not left a will, and so the rules of intestate succession apply.
- In determining the inheritance rights of spouses, male and female surviving spouses do not have any living children.

For the questions on retirement and pensions, it is assumed that

- The woman gave birth without complications to two healthy children.
- The woman ceased all paid activity during periods of childcare. If the period covered by a pension credit is conditioned on the age of the child, the period until the child reaches age one is counted.
- If transitional provisions gradually change the retirement age, the answers reflect the retirement age as of October 1, 2022, even if the law provides for changes over time.
- If a mandatory contributory pension system applicable to the private sector and a noncontributory universal pension system coexist, the answers correspond to the rules applicable to the mandatory contributory pension system.
- If pension systems are not mandatory or were not operational as of October 1, 2022, they are not measured.

Mobility

The Mobility indicator measures constraints on a woman's agency and freedom of movement, both of which are likely to influence her decision to enter the labor force and engage in entrepreneurial activity (Htun, Jensenius, and Nelson-Nunez 2019). This indicator has four components that measure the following:

- **Whether a woman can choose where to live in the same way as a man**. A score of 1 is assigned if there are no restrictions on a woman choosing where to live. A score of 0 is assigned if there are legal restrictions on a woman choosing where to live, if the husband chooses the marital home or has more weight in determining where the family will live, or if a woman's domicile automatically follows that of her husband.

- **Whether a woman can travel outside her home in the same way as a man.** A score of 1 is assigned if there are no restrictions on a woman traveling alone domestically. A score of 0 is assigned if permission, additional documentation, or the presence of her husband or guardian is required for a woman to travel alone domestically. A score of 0 is also assigned if a woman must justify her reasons for leaving the home or if leaving the home without a valid reason is considered disobedience with legal consequences, such as loss of right to maintenance.

- **Whether a woman can apply for a passport in the same way as a man.** This question considers actual application forms and procedures available at the relevant agency or on official government websites, in addition to what the law specifies. A score of 1 is assigned if there are no gender differences in passport application procedures. A score of 0 is assigned if an adult woman needs the permission or signature of her husband, father, or other relative or guardian to apply for a passport. A score of 0 is also assigned if passport application procedures or forms require a woman to provide details about her husband, father, or other relative or guardian or additional documents such as a marriage certificate and if the same is not required of a man.

- **Whether a woman can travel outside the country in the same way as a man.** A score of 1 is assigned if there are no restrictions on a woman traveling alone internationally. A score of 0 is assigned if permission, additional documentation, or the presence of her husband or a guardian is required for a woman to leave the country. A score of 0 is also assigned if the law requires a married woman to accompany her husband out of the country if he wishes her to do so.

Workplace

The Workplace indicator analyzes laws affecting women's decisions to enter the labor market, including women's legal capacity and ability to work, as well as protections in the workplace against discrimination and sexual harassment. Antidiscrimination legislation is positively associated with women's employment and earnings, whereas sexual harassment can negatively influence women's career trajectories (Amin and Islam 2015; Cavalcanti and Tavares 2016; McLaughlin, Uggen, and Blackstone 2017). This indicator has four components that assess the following:

- **Whether a woman can get a job in the same way as a man.** A score of 1 is assigned if there are no restrictions on a woman's legal capacity and ability to get a job or pursue a trade or profession. A score of 0 is assigned if a husband can prevent his wife from working or if permission or additional documentation is required for a woman to work but not for a man. A score of 0 is also assigned if it is considered a form of disobedience with legal consequences, such as loss of maintenance, for a woman to work contrary to her husband's wishes or the interests of the family.

- **Whether the law prohibits discrimination in employment based on gender.** A score of 1 is assigned if the law prohibits employers from discriminating based on sex or gender or mandates equal treatment of women and men in employment. A score of 0 is assigned if the law does not prohibit such discrimination or only prohibits it in one aspect of employment, such as pay or dismissal.

- **Whether there is legislation on sexual harassment in employment.** A score of 1 is assigned if legal provisions specifically protect against sexual harassment in employment, including unwelcome verbal or physical conduct of a sexual nature. A score of 0 is assigned if there is no such legislation. A score of 0 is also assigned if the law addresses harassment in general but makes no reference to acts of a sexual nature or contact or if it states only that the employer has a duty to prevent sexual harassment and has no provisions prohibiting it or providing sanctions or other forms of redress.

- **Whether there are criminal penalties or civil remedies for sexual harassment in employment.** A score of 1 is assigned if the law establishes criminal sanctions, such as fines or imprisonment, for sexual harassment in employment. A score of 1 is also assigned if the criminal code provides for reparation or damages for offenses covered by the code or if the law provides for civil remedies or compensation for victims of sexual harassment in employment or the workplace, even after dismissal of the victim. A score of 0 is assigned if the law establishes neither criminal sanctions for sexual harassment in employment nor civil remedies or compensation for victims of sexual harassment in employment. A score of 0 is also assigned if the law only prohibits sexual harassment in employment and sets forth that the employer should apply discretionary sanctions.

Pay

The Pay indicator measures laws affecting occupational segregation and the gender wage gap. Restrictions on certain jobs have been found to be correlated negatively with female employment (Costa, Silva, and Vaz 2009; Ogloblin 2005; Scarborough 2020; World Bank 2012; Zveglich and van der Meulen Rodgers 2003). This indicator has four components that assess the following:

- **Whether the law mandates equal remuneration for work of equal value.** "Remuneration" refers to the ordinary, basic, or minimum wage or salary and any additional emoluments payable directly or indirectly, whether in cash or in kind, by the employer to the worker and arising from the worker's employment. "Work of equal value" refers not only to the same or similar jobs but also to different jobs of the same value. A score of 1 is assigned if employers are legally obliged to pay equal remuneration to male and female employees who perform work of equal value in accordance with these definitions. A score of 0 is assigned if the law limits the principle of equal remuneration to equal work, the same work, similar work, or work of a similar nature. A score of 0 is also assigned if the law limits the broad concept of "remuneration" to only basic wages or salary.

- **Whether a woman can work at night in the same way as a man.** A score of 1 is assigned if a woman who is not pregnant and not nursing can work at night in the same way as a man. A score of 1 is also assigned when restrictions on a woman's ability to work at night do not apply to the food retail sector, a woman's consent to work at night is required, or an employer needs to comply with safety measures (such as providing transportation). A score of 0 is assigned if the law broadly prohibits a woman, including one with children over the age of one, from working at night or limits the hours that she can work at night. A score of 0 is also assigned if the law gives the relevant authority the power to restrict or prohibit a woman's ability to work at night, regardless of any decisions issued by that authority.

- **Whether a woman can work in a job deemed dangerous in the same way as a man.** A score of 1 is assigned if no laws prohibit or restrict a woman who is not pregnant and not nursing from working in a broad and subjective category of jobs deemed hazardous, arduous, or morally inappropriate. A score of 0 is assigned if the law prohibits or restricts a woman's ability to work in jobs deemed hazardous, arduous, or morally inappropriate. A score of 0 is also assigned if the law gives the relevant authority the power to determine whether particular jobs are too hazardous, arduous, or morally inappropriate for a woman but not for a man, regardless of any decisions issued by that authority.

- **Whether a woman can work in an industrial job in the same way as a man.** A score of 1 is assigned if a woman who is not pregnant and not nursing can work in the mining, construction, manufacturing, energy, water, agriculture, and transportation industries in the same way as a man. A score of 0 is assigned if the law prohibits a woman from working in any of these industries. A score of 0 is also assigned if a woman's employment in the relevant industries is restricted in any way, such as by prohibiting her from working at night in "industrial undertakings" or by giving the relevant authority the power to prohibit or restrict her ability to work in certain jobs or industries, regardless of any decisions issued by that authority.

Marriage

The Marriage indicator measures legal constraints related to marriage and divorce. Legal discrimination against women, including limits on their ability to be head of household, has been found to be negatively correlated with labor force participation (Goldin and Olivetti 2013; Gonzales et al. 2015). Unequal rights in marriage and divorce can also have negative effects on a woman's intrahousehold bargaining power and jeopardize her financial security when a divorce is finalized (Voena 2015). This indicator has five components that measure the following:

- **Whether the law is free of any provisions that require a married woman to obey her husband.** A score of 1 is assigned if there is no provision requiring a married woman to obey her husband. A score of 0 is assigned if there is any provision stating that a married woman must obey her husband or if disobeying the husband has legal ramifications for a married woman, such as loss of her right to maintenance.

- **Whether a woman can be head of household in the same way as a man.** A score of 1 is assigned if there are no restrictions on a woman being head of household or head of family. A score of 0 is assigned if the law designates the husband as head of household or stipulates that he leads the family. A score of 0 is also assigned if a male is designated as the default family member who receives the family book or equivalent document that is needed for accessing services. Gender differences under tax law are not measured by this question.

- **Whether there is legislation specifically addressing domestic violence.** A score of 1 is assigned if there is legislation addressing domestic violence that includes criminal sanctions or provides for protection orders for domestic violence. A score of 0 is assigned if there is no legislation addressing domestic violence, if the domestic violence legislation does not provide for sanctions or protection orders, or if only a specific category of women or family member is protected. A score of 0 is also assigned if there is only a provision that increases penalties for general crimes covered in the criminal code if committed between spouses or within the family.

- **Whether a woman can obtain a judgment of divorce in the same way as a man.** A score of 1 is assigned if the process to obtain a judgment of divorce is equal for a woman and a man or provides additional protections for a woman, such as prohibiting a husband from initiating divorce proceedings while his wife is pregnant. A score of 0 is assigned if there are procedural or evidentiary differences for a woman, if only a man can initiate divorce proceedings, or if divorce is not legally allowed.

- **Whether a woman has the same right to remarry as a man.** A score of 1 is assigned if a woman and a man have equal rights to remarry. A score of 0 is assigned if the law limits a woman's right to remarry, such as by requiring a waiting period before remarriage to which a man is not subject. A score of 0 is also assigned if divorce is not legally allowed.

Parenthood

The Parenthood indicator examines laws affecting women's work during and after pregnancy. Women are more likely to return to work if the law mandates maternity leave (Berger and Waldfogel 2004). This indicator has five components that measure the following:

- **Whether paid leave of at least 14 weeks is available to mothers.** A score of 1 is assigned if mothers are legally entitled to at least 14 weeks (98 calendar days) of paid leave for the birth of a child through maternity leave, parental leave, or a combination of both. A score of 0 is assigned if the law does not establish paid leave for mothers or if the length of paid leave is less than 14 weeks.

- **Whether the government administers 100 percent of maternity leave benefits.** A score of 1 is assigned if leave benefits are fully administered by a government entity, including compulsory social insurance schemes (such as social security), public funds, government-mandated private insurance, or employer reimbursement of any maternity leave benefits paid directly to an employee. A score of 0 is assigned if any of the cost is shared by the employer. A score of 0 is also assigned if contributions or taxes are mandated only for female employees, if the social insurance scheme that provides maternity leave benefits is optional, or if no paid leave is available to expectant and new mothers.

- **Whether paid leave is available to fathers.** A score of 1 is assigned if fathers are legally entitled to at least one day of paid paternity leave for the birth of a child or if the law reserves a portion of paid parental leave specifically for fathers—that is, through "use-it-or-lose-it" policies or fathers' quotas. A score of 1 is also assigned if fathers are individually entitled to paid parental leave. A score of 0 is assigned if the law does not guarantee fathers any paid paternity leave or other specific leave for the birth of a child. A score of 0 is also assigned if allowances for the birth of a child must be deducted from annual or sick leave.

- **Whether there is paid parental leave.** A score of 1 is assigned if parents are legally entitled to some form of full-time paid parental leave, either shared between mother and father (at least two weeks) or as an individual entitlement that each can take regardless of the other (at least one week each). A score of 1 is also assigned if the duration of paid maternity leave and paid paternity leave is the same. A score of 0 is assigned if the law does not mandate any form of paid parental leave.

- **Whether dismissal of pregnant workers is prohibited.** A score of 1 is assigned if the law explicitly prohibits the dismissal of pregnant women, if pregnancy cannot serve as grounds for terminating a contract, or if dismissal of pregnant workers is considered a form of unlawful termination, unfair dismissal, or wrongful discharge. A score of 0 is assigned if there are no provisions prohibiting the dismissal of pregnant workers or if the law only prohibits the dismissal of pregnant workers during maternity leave, for a limited period of the pregnancy, or when pregnancy results in illness or disability.

Entrepreneurship

The Entrepreneurship indicator measures constraints on the ability of women to start and run a business. For example, having access to a bank account is strongly correlated with women's labor supply (Field et al. 2021; Gonzales et al. 2015; Islam, Muzi, and Amin 2019). This indicator has four components that measure the following:

- **Whether the law prohibits discrimination in access to credit based on gender.** A score of 1 is assigned if the law prohibits discrimination by creditors based on sex or gender or prescribes equal access for both men and women when conducting financial transactions or entrepreneurial activities. A score of 1 is also assigned if the law prohibits gender discrimination when accessing goods and services (and services are defined to include financial services). A score of 0 is assigned if the law does not prohibit such discrimination or if the law does not provide for effective remedies.

- **Whether a woman can sign a contract in the same way as a man.** A score of 1 is assigned if a woman obtains full legal capacity on reaching the age of majority and there are no restrictions on her signing legally binding contracts. A score of 0 is assigned if a woman has limited legal capacity to sign a contract or needs the signature, consent, or permission of her husband or guardian to do so.

- **Whether a woman can register a business in the same way as a man.** A score of 1 is assigned if there are no restrictions on a woman registering a business. A score of 0 is assigned if a woman has limited legal capacity, including situations in which she needs her husband's or guardian's permission, signature, or consent to register a business. A score of 0 is also assigned if the registration process at any stage requires a woman to provide additional information or documentation that is not required of a man.

- **Whether a woman can open a bank account in the same way as a man.** A score of 1 is assigned if there are no restrictions on a woman opening a bank account. A score of 0 is assigned if a woman has limited legal capacity or is required to provide any additional permission or documentation that is not required of a man. A score of 0 is also assigned if legal provisions limit the ability of a woman to open a bank account, such as by stating that only a married woman who is separately employed from her husband may open a bank account in her own name.

Assets

The Assets indicator examines gender differences in property and inheritance law, including instances in which legal systems are supported by customary law and judicial precedent. Improving property and inheritance rights is positively associated with female earnings and employment (Heath and Tan 2018; Peterman 2011) as well as with women's access to housing and land (Gaddis, Lahoti, and Swaminathan 2020). This indicator has five components that measure the following:

- **Whether men and women have equal ownership rights to immovable property.** A score of 1 is assigned if there are no restrictions on a woman's legal capacity and rights to immovable property. A score of 0 is assigned if a woman's rights to own or administer property are legally restricted. A score of 0 is also assigned if there are gender differences in the legal treatment of spousal property, such as granting the husband administrative control of marital property.

- **Whether sons and daughters have equal rights to inherit assets from their parents.** A score of 1 is assigned if sons and daughters have the same rights to inherit assets from their parents. A score of 0 is assigned if there are gender-based differences in the recognition of children as heirs to property.

- **Whether male and female surviving spouses have equal rights to inherit assets.** A score of 1 is assigned if surviving spouses of either gender with no living children have the same inheritance rights. A score of 0 is assigned if there are gender-based differences in the inheritance rights of surviving spouses.

- **Whether the law grants male and female spouses equal administrative authority over assets during marriage.** A score of 1 is assigned if spouses retain administrative power over the assets each brought to the marriage or acquired during the marriage and their accrued value without the need for spousal consent. A score of 1 is also assigned if spouses administer their separate property, but spousal consent is required for major transactions, such as selling or pledging the property as collateral, or if both spouses have equal rights in the administration and transaction of joint property. A score of 0 is assigned if the husband has administrative rights over marital property, including any separate property of the wife, or if the husband's word prevails in case of disagreement.

- **Whether the law provides for the valuation of nonmonetary contributions.** Nonmonetary contributions include caring for minor children, taking care of the family home, or any other nonmonetized contribution from a stay-at-home spouse. A score of 1 is assigned if there is an explicit legal recognition of such contributions and the law provides for equal or equitable division of the property or the transfer of a lump sum to the stay-at-home spouse based on nonmonetary contributions. A score of 1 is also assigned if the default marital property regime is full community, partial community, or deferred community of property because these regimes implicitly recognize nonmonetary contributions at the time of property division and benefit both spouses regardless of who purchased property or holds title to it. A score of 0 is assigned if the default marital property regime is not a form of community of property and there is no explicit legal provision providing for equal or equitable division of property based on nonmonetary contributions.

Pension

The Pension indicator assesses laws affecting the size of a woman's pension. Early retirement can widen the potential gender gap in pension levels and increase women's risk of poverty in old age (Burn et al. 2020; Chłoń-Domińczak 2017). This indicator has four components that measure the following:

- **Whether the age at which men and women can retire with full pension benefits is the same.** A score of 1 is assigned if the statutory age at which men and women can retire and receive an irrevocable minimum old-age pension is the same. A score of 0 is assigned if there is a difference in the statutory age or if there is no mandatory pension scheme implemented for private sector workers.

- **Whether the age at which men and women can retire with partial pension benefits is the same.** "Partial pension benefits" refer to a reduced or proportional minimum old-age pension payable to workers who did not accumulate enough work experience or periods of contribution or have not reached the statutory age to qualify for a minimum old-age pension. A score of 1 is assigned if the age at which men and women can retire and receive partial pension benefits is the same or if the age at which men and women can retire and receive partial benefits is not mandated. A score of 0 is assigned if the age at which men and women can retire and receive partial pension benefits is different or if there is no mandatory pension scheme implemented for private sector workers.

- **Whether the mandatory retirement age for men and women is the same.** A score of 1 is assigned if the legally established age at which men and women must retire is the same or if there is no mandatory retirement age. A score of 0 is assigned if the age at which men and women must retire is different.

- **Whether periods of absence from work due to childcare are accounted for in pension benefits.** A score of 1 is assigned if pension contributions are paid or credited during maternity or parental leave or the leave period is considered a qualifying period of employment used for the purpose of calculating pension benefits. A score of 1 is also assigned if there are mechanisms to compensate for any contribution gaps and to ensure that the leave period does not reduce the assessment base or pension amounts or if there are no mandatory contributory pension schemes, but there is a noncontributory universal social pension conditioned on noncontributory requirements with no means test attached. A score of 0 is assigned if there are no compensating pension arrangements for periods of childcare or if there is no mandatory contributory pension scheme for private sector workers and no noncontributory universal social pension.

Reforms and data updates

Each year, *Women, Business and the Law* indicators capture changes in domestic laws and regulations that affect women's economic opportunities. Summaries of such changes are listed in annex 1B, thereby acknowledging the legal reform efforts undertaken by governments during the period reviewed. Any legislative or regulatory change that positively affects the score assigned to a given economy on any question under the eight indicators is classified as a reform; when the change affects the score negatively, it is classified as a negative change.

For questions that refer to legal rights, the change must be mandatory, meaning that women can enforce their rights in court or sanctions can be leveled by a regulatory body such as a central bank, employment tribunal, national human rights commission, or other enforcement body, including the police. For questions that refer to benefits, such as maternity, parental, or pension benefits, women must be able to obtain the benefit as of the cutoff date of the report. Policies, guidelines, model rules, principles, and recommendations are excluded, as are ratified international conventions when they have not been incorporated into domestic law. Reforms affecting the *Women, Business and the Law* indicators include, but are not limited to, amendments to or the introduction of a new constitution, labor law, family or personal status law, penal code, or administrative procedures.

Data for all economies are reviewed by local respondents and verified with the corresponding basis by the *Women, Business and the Law* team annually. This review can lead to corrections of data as a result of new information obtained, clarifications of answers, or consistency checks. To provide a comparable time series for research, the data set is back-calculated to adjust for any revisions in data due to corrections.

Governments can submit queries on the data and provide new information to the *Women, Business and the Law* team. Together with the team's response, the submissions are available on the project website at https://wbl.worldbank.org.

Methodological changes

The *Women, Business and the Law* team periodically revises and implements changes to the methodology to ensure a rigorous analysis of laws and regulations. The following methodology changes, already announced in previous editions, will be implemented in *Women, Business and the Law 2024*:

- **Marriage.** The question of whether a woman is or is not legally required to obey her husband will be revised to capture all forms of implied obedience outlined in the law. Unequal bargaining power within the household puts married women at a disadvantage compared with married men. Currently the question only captures instances where the letter of the law explicitly refers to obedience. This approach does not account for instances where the law may not refer verbatim to the term "obedience" but may still legally require a wife to obey her husband, for example by imposing marital duties on the wife only.

- **Parenthood.** The provision of paid parental leave to working parents can positively affect women's labor market outcomes (Akgündüz and Plantenga 2013) and increase the support provided by fathers to mothers in caring for newborns (Rossin-Slater 2017). However, the design of leave policies matters more for gender equality than their mere existence (Brandth and Kvande 2018; Frodermann, Wrohlich, and Zucc 2020; Marynissen et al. 2019; Patnaik 2014). To reflect more closely the existence and design of paid leave policies for working parents around the world, *Women, Business and the Law* proposes merging the questions related to paid maternity leave, paid paternity leave, and paid parental leave into two questions that capture the existence of paid leave available to mothers and fathers and their respective length. *Women, Business and the Law* will therefore continue to research and consult with experts on this issue. This effort may lead to a rephrasing of the Parenthood indicator in the

2024 edition of the report to streamline the reporting on paid leave policies available to working parents around the world.

As the team plans to introduce new indicators on women's safety, access to childcare, and implementation, the methodology for other questions will be reviewed and potentially revised in the future. *Women, Business and the Law* aims to maintain the relevance of the methodology by updating it as necessary and preserving comparability over time by only reviewing the methodology at regular medium-term intervals. The process and timeline for methodological changes will follow the protocols established in the *Women, Business and the Law* manual and guide, available on the project's website, at https://wbl.worldbank.org/en/aboutus.

More detailed data on each economy included in this report appear on the project website at https://wbl.worldbank.org. The team welcomes feedback on the methodology and construction of this set of indicators and looks forward to improving their coverage and scope. Comments can be offered by contacting the *Women, Business and the Law* team at wbl@worldbank.org.

References

Akgündüz, Yusuf Emre, and Janneke Plantenga. 2013. "Labour Market Effects of Parental Leave in Europe." *Cambridge Journal of Economics* 37 (4): 845–62.

Amin, Mohammad, and Asif Islam. 2015. "Does Mandating Nondiscrimination in Hiring Practices Influence Women's Employment? Evidence Using Firm-Level Data." *Feminist Economics* 21 (4): 28–60.

Berger, Lawrence M., and Jane Waldfogel. 2004. "Maternity Leave and the Employment of New Mothers in the United States." *Journal of Population Economics* 17 (2): 331–49.

Brandth, Berit, and Elin Kvande. 2018. "Fathers' Sense of Entitlement to Ear-Marked and Shared Parental Leave." *Sociological Review* 67 (5): 1154–69.

Burn, Ian, Patrick Button, Theodore F. Figinski, and Joanne Song McLaughlin. 2020. "Why Retirement, Social Security, and Age Discrimination Policies Need to Consider the Intersectional Experiences of Older Women." *Public Policy and Aging Report* 30 (3): 101–06.

Cavalcanti, Tiago, and José Tavares. 2016. "The Output Cost of Gender Discrimination: A Model-Based Macroeconomics Estimate." *Economic Journal* 126 (590): 109–34. https://academic.oup.com/ej/article-abstract/126/590/109/5077422.

Chłoń-Domińczak, Agnieszka. 2017. "Gender Gap in Pensions: Looking Ahead." Study for the Femme Committee, Directorate-General for Internal Policies, European Parliament, Brussels.

Costa, Joana, Elydia Silva, and Fabio Vaz. 2009. "The Role of Gender Inequalities in Explaining Income Growth, Poverty, and Inequality: Evidence from Latin American Countries." Working Paper 52, International Policy Center for Inclusive Growth, Brasília.

Field, Erica, Rohini Pande, Natalia Rigol, Simone Schaner, and Charity Troyer Moore. 2021. "On Her Own Account: How Strengthening Women's Financial Control Impacts Labor Supply and Gender Norms." *American Economic Review* 111 (7): 2342–75.

Frodermann, Corinna, Katharina Wrohlich, and Aline Zucc. 2020. "Parental Leave Reform and Long-Run Earnings of Mothers." IZA Discussion Paper 12935, Institute of Labor Economics, Bonn.

Gaddis, Isis, Rahul Lahoti, and Hema Swaminathan. 2020. "Women's Legal Rights and Gender Gaps in Property Ownership in Developing Countries." Policy Research Working Paper 9444, World Bank, Washington, DC.

Goldin, Claudia, and Claudia Olivetti. 2013. "Shocking Labor Supply: A Reassessment of the Role of World War II on Women's Labor Supply." *American Economic Review* 103 (3): 257–62.

Gonzales, Christian, Sonali Jain-Chandra, Kalpana Kochhar, and Monique Newiak. 2015. "Fair Play: More Equal Laws Boost Female Labor Force Participation." IMF Staff Discussion Note SDN/15/02, International Monetary Fund, Washington, DC.

Heath, Rachel, and Xu Tan. 2018. "Intrahousehold Bargaining, Female Autonomy, and Labor Supply: Theory and Evidence from India." Working paper, Department of Economics, University of Washington, Seattle.

Htun, Mala, Francesca R. Jensenius, and Jami Nelson-Nunez. 2019. "Gender-Discriminatory Laws and Women's Economic Agency." *Social Politics: International Studies in Gender, State and Society* 26 (2): 193–222.

Islam, Asif, Silvia Muzi, and Mohammad Amin. 2019. "Unequal Laws and the Disempowerment of Women in the Labour Market: Evidence from Firm-Level Data." *Journal of Development Studies* 55 (5): 822–44.

Marynissen, Leen, Eleonora Mussino, Jonas Wood, and Ann-Zofie Duvander. 2019. "Fathers' Parental Leave Uptake in Belgium and Sweden: Self-Evident or Subject to Employment Characteristics?" *Social Sciences* 8 (11): 312.

McLaughlin, Heather, Christopher Uggen, and Amy Blackstone. 2017. "The Economic and Career Effects of Sexual Harassment on Working Women." *Gender and Society* 31 (3): 333–58.

Ogloblin, Constantin G. 2005. "The Gender Earnings Differential in Russia after a Decade of Economic Transition." *Applied Econometrics and International Development* 5 (3): 5–26.

Patnaik, Ankita. 2014. "Making Leave Easier: Better Compensation and Daddy-Only Entitlements." Working paper, Cornell University, Ithaca, NY.

Peterman, Amber. 2011. "Women's Property Rights and Gendered Policies: Implications for Women's Long-Term Welfare in Rural Tanzania." *Journal of Development Studies* 47 (1): 1–30.

Rossin-Slater, Maya. 2017. "Maternity and Family Leave Policy." NBER Working Paper w23069, National Bureau of Economic Research, Cambridge, MA.

Scarborough, William J. 2020. "Occupational Gender Segregation and Economic Growth in US Local Labor Markets, 1980 through 2010." *PloS One* 15 (1): e0227615.

Voena, Alessandra. 2015. "Yours, Mine, and Ours: Do Divorce Laws Affect the Intertemporal Behavior of Married Couples?" *American Economic Review* 105 (8): 2295–332.

World Bank. 2012. *World Development Report 2012: Gender Equality and Development*. Washington, DC: World Bank. https://openknowledge.worldbank.org/handle/10986/4391.

Zveglich, Joseph E., and Yana van der Meulen Rodgers. 2003. "The Impact of Protective Measures for Female Workers." *Journal of Labor Economics* 21 (3): 533–55.

APPENDIX B | Economy Data

Table B.1 captures legal differences between men and women on eight economy-level indicators that comprise the *Women, Business and the Law* index.

TABLE B.1	ECONOMY-LEVEL INDICATOR DATA								
Economy	Main business city	MOBILITY	WORKPLACE	PAY	MARRIAGE	PARENTHOOD	ENTREPRENEUR-SHIP	ASSETS	PENSION	WBL 2023 INDEX
Afghanistan	Kabul	25	50	0	20	20	75	40	25	31.9
Albania	Tirana	100	100	100	100	80	100	100	50	91.3
Algeria	Algiers	75	75	50	60	60	75	40	25	57.5
Angola	Luanda	100	100	50	100	60	100	100	25	79.4
Antigua and Barbuda	St. John's	75	50	75	100	0	75	80	75	66.3
Argentina	Buenos Aires (Ciudad autonoma de)	100	75	50	100	60	75	100	75	79.4
Armenia	Yerevan	100	50	75	100	100	75	100	100	87.5
Australia	Sydney	100	100	100	100	100	100	100	75	96.9
Austria	Vienna	100	100	100	100	100	100	100	75	96.9
Azerbaijan	Baku	100	100	0	100	80	100	100	50	78.8
Bahamas, The	Nassau	100	100	75	80	20	75	100	100	81.3
Bahrain	Manama	50	75	100	40	40	100	40	100	68.1
Bangladesh	Dhaka	100	50	25	60	20	75	40	25	49.4
Barbados	Bridgetown	75	100	50	100	40	75	100	100	80.0
Belarus	Minsk	100	50	50	100	80	75	100	50	75.6
Belgium	Brussels	100	100	100	100	100	100	100	100	100.0
Belize	Belize City	75	75	50	100	60	75	100	100	79.4
Benin	Cotonou	75	100	75	80	60	100	80	100	83.8
Bhutan	Thimphu	100	100	100	80	40	75	80	25	75.0
Bolivia	La Paz	100	75	100	100	60	100	100	75	88.8
Bosnia and Herzegovina	Sarajevo	100	100	50	100	80	100	100	50	85.0
Botswana	Gaborone	75	25	75	100	0	75	60	100	63.8
Brazil	São Paulo	100	100	75	100	80	75	100	50	85.0
Brunei Darussalam	Bandar Seri Begawan	50	25	75	40	0	75	60	100	53.1
Bulgaria	Sofia	100	100	100	100	100	100	100	25	90.6
Burkina Faso	Ouagadougou	75	100	25	80	80	100	100	100	82.5

(Table continues next page)

TABLE B.1	ECONOMY-LEVEL INDICATOR DATA *(continued)*								
Economy	Main business city	MOBILITY	WORKPLACE	PAY	MARRIAGE	PARENTHOOD	ENTREPRENEUR-SHIP	ASSETS	PENSION	WBL 2023 INDEX
Burundi	Bujumbura	100	100	100	60	40	75	60	75	76.3
Cabo Verde	Praia	100	100	75	100	40	100	100	75	86.3
Cambodia	Phnom Penh	100	100	75	80	20	100	100	75	81.3
Cameroon	Douala	50	75	25	40	80	50	60	100	60.0
Canada	Toronto	100	100	100	100	100	100	100	100	100.0
Central African Republic	Bangui	75	100	25	80	60	75	100	100	76.9
Chad	N'Djamena	75	75	50	60	60	50	60	100	66.3
Chile	Santiago	100	75	75	80	100	75	60	75	80.0
China	Shanghai	100	100	25	100	100	75	100	25	78.1
Colombia	Bogotá	100	100	50	100	100	75	100	50	84.4
Comoros	Moroni	75	75	100	40	40	75	40	75	65.0
Congo, Dem. Rep.	Kinshasa	100	100	50	40	80	100	60	100	78.8
Congo, Rep.	Brazzaville	50	75	25	60	20	75	60	100	58.1
Costa Rica	San José	100	100	100	100	60	75	100	100	91.9
Côte d'Ivoire	Abidjan	100	100	100	80	80	100	100	100	95.0
Croatia	Zagreb	100	100	100	100	100	100	100	50	93.8
Cyprus	Nicosia	100	100	75	100	80	100	100	100	94.4
Czechia	Prague	100	100	100	100	100	100	100	50	93.8
Denmark	Copenhagen	100	100	100	100	100	100	100	100	100.0
Djibouti	Djibouti Ville	100	100	50	20	60	100	40	100	71.3
Dominica	Roseau	75	25	50	100	0	75	100	75	62.5
Dominican Republic	Santo Domingo	100	100	75	80	60	100	100	75	86.3
Ecuador	Quito	100	100	100	100	40	75	100	100	89.4
Egypt, Arab Rep.	Cairo	50	75	0	20	20	100	40	100	50.6
El Salvador	San Salvador	100	100	75	80	80	100	100	75	88.8
Equatorial Guinea	Malabo	75	25	100	20	60	0	60	75	51.9
Eritrea	Asmara	100	100	75	60	20	75	100	25	69.4
Estonia	Tallinn	100	100	100	80	100	100	100	100	97.5
Eswatini	Mbabane	100	25	50	40	20	0	60	75	46.3
Ethiopia	Addis Ababa	100	100	25	80	60	75	100	75	76.9
Fiji	Suva	100	100	50	100	60	75	100	75	82.5
Finland	Helsinki	100	100	100	100	80	100	100	100	97.5
France	Paris	100	100	100	100	100	100	100	100	100.0
Gabon	Libreville	100	100	100	80	80	100	100	100	95.0
Gambia, The	Banjul	100	50	75	60	60	75	60	75	69.4
Georgia	Tbilisi	100	100	75	100	80	100	100	50	88.1

(Table continues next page)

TABLE B.1	ECONOMY-LEVEL INDICATOR DATA *(continued)*								
Economy	Main business city	MOBILITY	WORKPLACE	PAY	MARRIAGE	PARENTHOOD	ENTREPRENEUR-SHIP	ASSETS	PENSION	WBL 2023 INDEX
Germany	Berlin	100	100	100	100	100	100	100	100	100.0
Ghana	Accra	100	100	50	100	20	75	80	75	75.0
Greece	Athens	100	100	100	100	100	100	100	100	100.0
Grenada	St. George's	100	50	100	100	20	75	100	100	80.6
Guatemala	Guatemala City	100	25	50	80	60	75	100	100	73.8
Guinea	Conakry	100	100	50	60	20	100	60	100	73.8
Guinea-Bissau	Bissau	75	25	0	60	20	25	60	75	42.5
Guyana	Georgetown	75	100	100	80	40	100	100	100	86.9
Haiti	Port au Prince	50	50	100	40	40	75	60	75	61.3
Honduras	Tegucigalpa	100	100	50	80	20	100	100	50	75.0
Hong Kong SAR, China	Hong Kong	100	100	75	100	60	100	100	100	91.9
Hungary	Budapest	100	100	75	100	100	100	100	100	96.9
Iceland	Reykjavik	100	100	100	100	100	100	100	100	100.0
India	Mumbai	100	100	25	100	40	75	80	75	74.4
Indonesia	Jakarta	100	100	75	40	40	75	60	75	70.6
Iran, Islamic Rep.	Tehran	0	0	50	0	60	75	40	25	31.3
Iraq	Baghdad	25	100	50	0	20	100	40	50	48.1
Ireland	Dublin	100	100	100	100	100	100	100	100	100.0
Israel	Tel Aviv	100	100	50	60	60	100	100	75	80.6
Italy	Rome	100	100	100	80	100	100	100	100	97.5
Jamaica	Kingston	100	75	50	100	20	75	100	75	74.4
Japan	Tokyo	100	50	25	80	100	75	100	100	78.8
Jordan	Amman	25	0	75	20	40	100	40	75	46.9
Kazakhstan	Almaty	100	50	75	100	80	75	100	25	75.6
Kenya	Nairobi	100	100	100	100	40	50	80	75	80.6
Kiribati	Tarawa	100	100	100	100	20	75	40	75	76.3
Korea, Rep.	Seoul	100	100	25	100	80	75	100	100	85.0
Kosovo	Pristina	100	100	100	100	60	100	100	75	91.9
Kuwait	Kuwait City	50	50	0	40	0	75	40	25	35.0
Kyrgyz Republic	Bishkek	100	100	25	100	40	100	100	50	76.9
Lao PDR	Vientiane	100	100	75	100	80	100	100	50	88.1
Latvia	Riga	100	100	100	100	100	100	100	100	100.0
Lebanon	Beirut	100	100	50	60	20	75	40	25	58.8
Lesotho	Maseru	100	75	75	80	20	75	100	100	78.1
Liberia	Monrovia	100	100	100	100	20	75	80	75	81.3
Libya	Tripoli	75	50	75	20	40	75	40	25	50.0

(Table continues next page)

TABLE B.1	ECONOMY-LEVEL INDICATOR DATA *(continued)*								
Economy	**Main business city**	**MOBILITY**	**WORKPLACE**	**PAY**	**MARRIAGE**	**PARENTHOOD**	**ENTREPRENEUR-SHIP**	**ASSETS**	**PENSION**	**WBL 2023 INDEX**
Lithuania	Vilnius	100	100	100	100	100	100	100	50	93.8
Luxembourg	Luxembourg	100	100	100	100	100	100	100	100	100.0
Madagascar	Antananarivo	75	100	25	80	40	75	60	100	69.4
Malawi	Blantyre	50	100	100	100	40	75	100	75	80.0
Malaysia	Kuala Lumpur	50	50	50	40	0	75	60	75	50.0
Maldives	Malé	100	100	75	60	40	100	40	75	73.8
Mali	Bamako	75	50	50	20	60	75	80	100	63.8
Malta	Valletta	100	100	75	100	80	100	100	75	91.3
Marshall Islands	Majuro	100	50	100	100	0	100	0	75	65.6
Mauritania	Nouakchott	100	25	25	0	60	75	0	100	48.1
Mauritius	Port Louis	100	100	100	80	60	100	100	75	89.4
Mexico	Mexico City	100	100	75	100	60	100	100	75	88.8
Micronesia, Fed. Sts.	Island of Pohnpei (Palikir/Kolonia)	100	25	75	100	0	75	40	75	61.3
Moldova	Chisinau	100	75	100	100	100	100	100	25	87.5
Mongolia	Ulan Bator	100	100	100	100	100	100	100	25	90.6
Montenegro	Podgorica	100	100	50	100	80	100	100	50	85.0
Morocco	Casablanca	100	100	50	60	80	100	40	75	75.6
Mozambique	Maputo	100	100	50	100	60	100	100	50	82.5
Myanmar	Yangon	75	25	50	80	60	75	80	25	58.8
Namibia	Windhoek	75	100	100	100	40	75	100	100	86.3
Nepal	Kathmandu	75	100	100	100	40	75	80	75	80.6
Netherlands	Amsterdam	100	100	100	100	100	100	100	100	100.0
New Zealand	Auckland	100	100	100	100	80	100	100	100	97.5
Nicaragua	Managua	100	100	75	100	40	100	100	75	86.3
Niger	Niamey	75	75	75	20	60	50	0	100	56.9
Nigeria	Lagos	75	75	50	100	0	75	80	75	66.3
North Macedonia	Skopje	100	100	50	100	80	100	100	50	85.0
Norway	Oslo	100	100	100	100	100	75	100	100	96.9
Oman	Muscat	25	75	25	20	0	75	40	50	38.8
Pakistan	Karachi	75	100	50	60	20	75	40	50	58.8
Palau	Koror	100	25	75	100	0	75	0	75	56.3
Panama	Panama City	100	100	50	80	80	75	100	50	79.4
Papua New Guinea	Port Moresby	75	50	25	100	0	75	80	75	60.0
Paraguay	Asuncion	100	100	100	100	80	100	100	75	94.4
Peru	Lima	100	100	100	80	80	100	100	100	95.0
Philippines	Quezon City	75	100	100	60	60	100	60	75	78.8

(Table continues next page)

TABLE B.1	ECONOMY-LEVEL INDICATOR DATA *(continued)*								
Economy	Main business city	MOBILITY	WORKPLACE	PAY	MARRIAGE	PARENTHOOD	ENTREPRENEUR-SHIP	ASSETS	PENSION	WBL 2023 INDEX
Poland	Warsaw	100	100	100	100	100	100	100	50	93.8
Portugal	Lisbon	100	100	100	100	100	100	100	100	100.0
Puerto Rico (US)	San Juan	100	100	75	100	20	100	100	75	83.8
Qatar	Doha	25	0	50	20	0	75	40	25	29.4
Romania	Bucharest	100	100	100	100	100	100	100	25	90.6
Russian Federation	Moscow	100	50	50	80	80	75	100	50	73.1
Rwanda	Kigali	100	100	100	100	20	75	100	75	83.8
Samoa	Apia	75	100	75	100	40	75	60	75	75.0
San Marino	San Marino	100	50	75	80	60	75	100	100	80.0
São Tomé and Príncipe	São Tomé	100	100	75	80	60	75	100	75	83.1
Saudi Arabia	Riyadh	50	100	100	40	40	100	40	100	71.3
Senegal	Dakar	75	100	50	60	80	75	40	100	72.5
Serbia	Belgrade	100	100	100	100	100	100	100	50	93.8
Seychelles	Victoria	75	50	75	100	80	75	80	75	76.3
Sierra Leone	Freetown	100	75	50	100	0	100	80	75	72.5
Singapore	Singapore	100	75	75	100	60	75	100	75	82.5
Slovak Republic	Bratislava	100	100	75	100	80	100	100	25	85.0
Slovenia	Ljubljana	100	100	75	100	100	100	100	100	96.9
Solomon Islands	Honiara	75	25	25	100	0	75	80	75	56.9
Somalia	Mogadishu	75	50	50	20	40	75	40	25	46.9
South Africa	Johannesburg	100	100	100	100	80	100	100	25	88.1
South Sudan	Juba	100	100	100	80	40	75	20	25	67.5
Spain	Madrid	100	100	100	100	100	100	100	100	100.0
Sri Lanka	Colombo	100	75	25	100	20	75	80	50	65.6
St. Kitts and Nevis	Basseterre	100	25	50	100	40	75	80	100	71.3
St. Lucia	Castries	75	100	100	80	40	75	100	100	83.8
St. Vincent and the Grenadines	Kingstown	75	25	50	100	20	75	100	100	68.1
Sudan	Khartoum	0	0	0	0	20	75	40	100	29.4
Suriname	Paramaribo	100	50	75	80	60	50	100	75	73.8
Sweden	Stockholm	100	100	100	100	100	100	100	100	100.0
Switzerland	Zurich	100	100	100	100	80	75	100	50	88.1
Syrian Arab Republic	Damascus	50	25	0	40	40	75	40	50	40.0

(Table continues next page)

TABLE B.1	ECONOMY-LEVEL INDICATOR DATA *(continued)*								
Economy	Main business city	MOBILITY	WORKPLACE	PAY	MARRIAGE	PARENTHOOD	ENTREPRENEUR-SHIP	ASSETS	PENSION	WBL 2023 INDEX
Taiwan, China	Taipei	100	100	100	100	80	75	100	75	91.3
Tajikistan	Dushanbe	100	50	50	100	80	100	100	50	78.8
Tanzania	Dar es Salaam	100	100	100	80	60	75	60	75	81.3
Thailand	Bangkok	100	100	75	80	20	75	100	75	78.1
Timor-Leste	Dili	100	75	100	80	60	75	100	100	86.3
Togo	Lomé	100	100	100	60	40	75	80	100	81.9
Tonga	Nukualofa	100	25	75	100	0	75	20	75	58.8
Trinidad and Tobago	Port of Spain	75	50	75	80	20	100	100	100	75.0
Tunisia	Tunis	100	75	25	60	40	75	40	100	64.4
Türkiye	Istanbul	100	100	75	80	80	75	100	50	82.5
Uganda	Kampala	100	100	100	80	40	75	80	75	81.3
Ukraine	Kyiv	100	100	0	100	80	100	100	100	85.0
United Arab Emirates	Dubai	100	100	100	60	60	100	40	100	82.5
United Kingdom	London	100	100	100	100	80	100	100	100	97.5
United States	New York City	100	100	75	100	80	100	100	75	91.3
Uruguay	Montevideo	100	100	75	80	80	75	100	100	88.8
Uzbekistan	Tashkent	100	50	25	80	60	100	100	50	70.6
Vanuatu	Port Vila	75	25	50	80	0	100	40	75	55.6
Venezuela, RB	Caracas	100	100	75	100	80	75	100	50	85.0
Vietnam	Ho Chi Minh City	100	100	100	100	80	100	100	25	88.1
West Bank and Gaza	Ramallah	25	25	0	20	0	75	40	25	26.3
Yemen, Rep.	Sanaa	25	25	25	0	0	75	40	25	26.9
Zambia	Lusaka	75	100	100	80	40	100	80	75	81.3
Zimbabwe	Harare	100	100	75	80	40	100	100	100	86.9

Source: Women, Business and the Law database.

www.ingramcontent.com/pod-product-compliance
Lightning Source LLC
Chambersburg PA
CBHW041446210326
41599CB00004B/152